By Order of His Excellency Guy Lord Dorchester

Captain General & Governor in Chief of the Provinces of Upper & Lower Can.

PLAN

REFERENCES

THE EASTERN TOWNSHIPS

A PICTORIAL RECORD

THE EASTERN TOWNSHIPS

A PICTORIAL RECORD

HISTORICAL PRINTS AND ILLUSTRATIONS OF THE
EASTERN TOWNSHIPS
OF THE
PROVINCE OF QUEBEC
CANADA

Charles P. deVolpi, F R P.S L and P. H. Scowen, D C L.

DEV-SCO PUBLICATIONS LTD.
MONTREAL, CANADA

v

f F̶L̶A̶S̶L̶

Dust Jacket and Book
designed by
W H Cripps

Printed by
Page-Sangster Printing Company Limited
Sherbrooke Que

ONULP

FOREWORD

In the last twenty years there has been a remarkable rise of interest in old Canadian prints Before that time there were a few keen and informed collectors. But the interest in old Canadian prints is now wide and active.

The explanation is clear. Within these same twenty years there has been an upsurge of Canadian consciousness. It has brought with it a curiosity to know how the country appeared in the days that are gone. There are many accounts written by those who lived in the various regions of Canada, or who travelled through them. These, too, are being more and more valued. But they do not quite meet the wish not only to read of former times but to see them with the eyes of the past.

This is a wish that old prints can fully satisfy. The artists' sketches and paintings, through the print-maker's skill, bring to life places as they once were. The present Canadian scene takes on deeper meaning when it is known how time has changed it, as it will change it again, as the present, in its turn, takes its place in the past.

In this book Mr. Charles deVolpi and Mr. Philip H. Scowen have carried out a most timely and useful service to history by drawing up a catalogue, with their notes and comments, of the prints of the Eastern Townships published between the 1830's and the 1880's. As 121 of these prints have been reproduced, the reader of the book may view this part of Canada in a new dimension, going back through time itself.

The half-century covered by this book was one alive with change. At the beginning of this period the Eastern Townships were part of the old colony of Lower Canada. During the middle years they were part of the new colony formed when Upper and Lower Canada were joined under a single government. In the last years of the period the Townships became part of the Province of Quebec in the new Dominion of Canada.

This rapid pace of constitutional development was matched by changes in many other ways. In these fifty active years the Townships developed their agriculture, their industries, their railways, their churches, schools and colleges They even had their own battlefield (as these prints show) in the Fenian Raid of 1870.

It was also a great half-century in the history of prints. In the 1830's photography was unknown, and the various types of prints were the only means of publishing the artist's work. During this period photography was invented The print, however, held much of its importance, though photography was rivalling it as a swifter means of capturing the face of the countryside.

Yet the old prints have qualities that photographs cannot provide. They not only depict scenery, buildings and people; they reveal them in the manner and fashion of the period. The prints themselves are period pieces, quite as much as what they record. And they are of interest, not least, for the way each reveals something of the artist whose work they reproduce.

Mr. deVolpi and Mr. Scowen have added greatly to the value of their book by carrying out their researches into the lives of the artists who worked in the Townships.

These artists cover a wide range. They include such figures of world fame as the English artist, W. H. Bartlett, who sketched not only in the Townships but elsewhere in Canada, as well as in the United States, Scotland, Ireland, Germany, and the Middle East, and who died on a journey in the Mediterranean.

Most notable among the Canadian artists of the Townships was Allan Edson, who was born on Stanbridge Ridge, and died at Glen Sutton, and who was one of the original members of the Royal Canadian Academy.

To these artists of fame must be added many others who have themselves faded into obscurity, though leaving work still fresh and clear. Mr. de Volpi and Mr. Scowen have gathered up the forgotten facts about these men and have increased immensely the value of their book as a permanent source of reference.

The compilation of this book — both in locating the prints and in providing the reading matter about them — has been a formidable task. Mr. deVolpi and Mr. Scowen have carried out their painstaking work in libraries, museums, art galleries, archives, the collections of historical societies and in private collections. Their aim has been to make their book as comprehensive as possible.

The patience needed to bring such a task to completion has been sustained by their zest, and rewarded by their discoveries. As a work of scholarship it commands respect, and it will hold an endless attraction for picturing the past as the past pictured itself. The result has been a contribution — and an important and enduring one — to appreciating one of the most picturesque, varied and historic regions of Canada.

EDGAR A. COLLARD.

PREFACE

This book is a compilation of the early prints of the Eastern Townships of the Province of Quebec. They are reproduced from woodcuts, engravings and lithographs of importance which were published over a period of approximately fifty years, from the earliest known in 1832.

A debt of gratitude is owed to the artists, engravers and publishers, as well as to the museums, archives and collectors, who have cherished them over the years.

It is unfortunate that space does not permit portraits of many other personages whose names and deeds were prominent in the early history of the Eastern Townships. Several areas have not been included This is because no prints have been located.

The spelling on the prints may not agree with today's spelling of some of the place names. However, they are shown as they appeared on the originals The descriptive wording facing each print has been taken verbatim from publications of the time, and it is hoped they will be of interest in spite of obvious inaccuracies and errors.

Many of the finest pictures were done by artists of the Eastern Townships — C. B. Felton, Mrs. J. V. Cooke, G. J. Bompas, W. S. Hunter, Jr., and Allan Edson. Although the latter two are comparatively well known, nothing has been written about the others. We hope that the short biographies included will prove of interest

Nearly half of the prints shown have never been included in any of the catalogues of Canadian prints and illustrations.

We hope that this volume of prints will illustrate the charm of the area referred to by General Alured Clarke, Lieutenant Governor of Lower Canada (1791-1796), as the "waste lands of the Crown."

ACKNOWLEDGMENTS

It is a great pleasure and satisfaction to express our gratitude and appreciation to the persons named below who have so generously given of their time and knowledge, and loaned prized possessions to use as we saw fit.

In collecting material we have received ready and willing assistance from everyone approached. To all these our sincere thanks is tendered.

Bernard Amtmann
Arnold Banfill
Jules Bazin
A. E. Bartlett
R. O. Bartlett
D'Arcy Bennett
Homer Blackwood
J. G. G. Bompas
Charles C. Colby
Edgar A. Collard
Mrs. Edgar A. Collard
William H. Cripps

Edgar Davidson
Mrs. Isobel Dobell
Mrs. Charles P. deVolpi
Miss Warda Drummond
Mrs. Harold V. Fellows
J. Douglas Ferguson
Royce L. Gale
Russell Harper
B. N. Holtham
Laurence M. Lande
Dr. W. Kaye Lamb
Miss Emily LeBaron

F. G. LeBaron
Father Leon Marcotte
Sherman Molony
Msgr. Maurice O'Bready
John L. Russell
F. J. Sangster
Mrs. P. H. Scowen
Reed Scowen
E. H. Spencer
F. St. George Spendlove
Edward J. Struthers
William P. Wolfe

INSTITUTIONS

Bishop's University
Brome County Historical Society
Town of Lennoxville
Mississquoi Historical Society
Bibliothèque Municipale (Cité de Montréal)
McCord Museum
McGill University

The National Gallery of Canada
Public Archives of Canada
The Royal Ontario Museum
Southern Canada Power
Stanstead Historical Society
La Société d'Histoire des Cantons de l'Est
Séminaire de Sherbrooke

CONTENTS

PLATES

THE ARTISTS AND ENGRAVERS

BARTLETT, WILLIAM HENRY (1809-1854) Born in London, England, March 26, 1809. Between 1836 and 1852 he made four trips to Canada and the United States. The drawings of Canada made on these trips were published in conjunction with N. P. Willis under the title Canadian Scenery Illustrated, London, 1842. They are a major contribution to Canada's Pictorial History. He died at sea, between Malta and Marseilles on September 14, 1854.

BOMPAS, DR. G. J (1812-1889) Born in Bristol, England on September 6th, 1812. Studied medicine in Cambridge and Edinburgh, F.R.C.S. Married Marianne Bedomme in 1838. They had twelve children. Came to Canada in 1860 and settled in Bury Township, did not practice medicine. Taught Botany and Art at Stanstead College and Bishop's College. He did a great many drawings and paintings of the Eastern Townships. Died at Lennoxville on June 23, 1889.

BOUCHETTE, JOSEPH, LT.-COL. (1774-1841) Born at Quebec, L.C., May 14, 1774, the son of Jean Baptiste Bouchette. About 1790 he entered the office of his uncle, Samuel Holland, Surveyor-General of Canada. In 1804 he succeeded to that office. He did all of the drawings for his own books in conjunction with his son R. S. M. Bouchette, also did the illustrations for the British American Land Company. He died at Montreal April 9, 1841.

BOUCHETTE, ROBERT SHORE MILNES (1805-1879) Born in Quebec March 2, 1805, the fourth and youngest son of Joseph Bouchette. He studied art under his father and did a lot of work with him. He was called to the Bar of Lower Canada in 1826, and he joined the ranks of the "patriots." He was implicated in the rebellion of 1837 and was banished to Bermuda. On his return to Canada under the amnesty he went into civil service. He died at Quebec June 4, 1879.

COOKE, MRS. J. V. (18—-1885) Wife of John Valentine Cooke Jr., nee Jane Ann Millar, daughter of Robert J. Millar and Eliza Robins, and the grand daughter of William Robins and James Millar, both officers of the British Army who settled in Drummondville in 1815 when the village was founded by Major General Heriot. Her husband operated a saw mill on the north side of the St. Francis River in Drummondville and they resided in a house situated opposite the present dam of the Southern Canada Power Company. Died at Drummondville about 1885.

EDSON, ALLAN (1846-1888) Landscape painter, was born at Stanbridge, Missisquoi County in 1846. He studied painting in Paris, France, under Pelouse; and on his return to Canada he became a charter member of the Royal Canadian Academy, 1880. Did considerable work in the Eastern Townships. Also Founding Member of the Society of Canadian Artists, 1867. Two of his paintings were bought by the Princess Louise and given to Queen Victoria. He died at Glen Sutton in 1888.

FELTON, CHARLES BRIDGMAN (1790-18—-) Born in England 1790. Married Henrietta Sexton in 1819. He had two sons, born in England between 1837 and 1840. He was first prothonotary in District of St. Francis. He was living in New York City from 1850 to 1863. He worked both as a lithographer and artist.

GASCARD, G. This artist did some work for the Canadian Illustrated News, and is listed in G. Morrisset's "La Peinture Traditionnelle au Canada Français" as a minor artist living in Montreal at the beginning of this century.

HABERER, EUGENE Was staff artist and engraver with the Canadian Illustrated News.

HUNTER, WILLIAM S. JR. (1823-1894) Was born at St. John's, Quebec in 1823. He married Miss Nancy Parsons of Stanstead and had two daughters and one son. In the Canada Directory of 1857-58 he was listed as an artist, illustrator and designer. In 1867 he was listed as a mining broker and in 1875 as a manufacturer of boots, shoes and harness. He died November 29, 1894 and is buried in Stanstead.

SANDHAM, HENRY (1842-1910) Painter and illustrator. Born in Montreal May 24, 1842. Son of John Sandham and Elizabeth Tait, younger brother of Alfred Sandham. Charter Member of the Royal Canadian Academy of Arts (1880). Worked at Notman's Photographic Studios in Montreal and was there associated with John A. Fraser, Adolphe Vogt, and other artists Founding Member of the Society of Canadian Artists, 1867. Later he went to England where he died neglected.

SCHEUER, W. (1872-1883) Prominent staff artist and engraver with the Canadian Illustrated News.

TURNER, E A Did the lithographs for Belden's Illustrated Atlas of Canada We have been unable to locate anything regarding him

VOGT, ADOLPHE (1842-1871) Born in Germany November 29, 1842. Came to America in 1846 and settled in Philadelphia where he received his first lessons in art He returned to Germany in 1861 and continued his studies until 1865 when he came to Montreal. During the Fenian Raids of 1870 he went to the front as a special artist for the Canadian Illustrated News He was also a very talented musician. He went to New York in December of 1870 and was struck down with Small Pox and died February 22nd, 1871.

WALKER, JOHN HENRY (1831-1899) Born in County Antrim, Ireland. Emigrated to Montreal 1852 where he listed himself as a landscape and portrait painter; and engraver on copper and wood. (Did considerable work for The Canadian Illustrated News, L'Opinion Publique, etc) died at Montreal June, 1899.

WELLGE, H. This artist did the "Bird s Eye Views" of Bedford, Coaticook, Lennoxville, Rock Island, Sherbrooke and Waterloo He also did views of Seattle and Tacoma, Washington Territory dated 1884.

WESTON, JAMES (1815-1896) Born about 1815. Painter — exhibited at the Society of Canadian Artists, Montreal 1867, at the Society of Canadian Artists, 1868-1879, and at the Royal Canadian Academy, 1880-90. He was elected an associate of the Royal Canadian Academy 1880 or 1882 and was still living in Montreal in 1886. In an article in 1893, he is referred to as an ex-patriot Canadian. He painted still life, portraits and landscapes in oil.

WISEMAN, JAMES LOVELL (1847-1912) Born at Montreal February 16, 1847. Worked as wood engraver in Montreal in the 1870's. Was a partner of John Henry Walker in 1875 and was listed in Montreal Directory as an engraver in 1896. He died January 13, 1912.

THE EASTERN TOWNSHIPS

WHAT are the Eastern Townships? The question may seem superfluous Nevertheless, many-residents of the area do not know the answer. The land included in the Eastern Townships is not separated by any natural features from other portions of the Province or from the adjacent States of Vermont, New Hampshire and Maine.

In general, the territorial clauses of the treaty which ended the American Revolution defined the southern boundary and the patterns of early French settlements determined the north, east and west boundaries of the Eastern Townships. The following pages recount some of the more important historical considerations which give a better understanding of the area.

When the French first seriously undertook to settle New France, they had at their disposal a vast area of accessible land along the banks of navigable waters. Many thousands of acres bordering the St. Lawrence, the Ottawa, the Richelieu, the Yamaska and the Chaudiere Rivers were well suited to cultivation without the necessity of building expensive roads through the wilderness. Hence, the French made grants along these streams.

Settlements in the remote and hilly regions of this area were dangerous and impractical because it was much too easy for raiding bands of hostile Iroquois to attack isolated settlements and get safely away before any action could be taken against them. Hence, the hinterland remained untouched and served only as a hunting ground for the Indians. This was the land which subsequently formed a large part of the Eastern Townships.

Therefore, at the time of the British Conquest (1759) the new masters of Canada found much barren country. They also found a system of land tenure fundamentally different from that to which

they were accustomed in their own colonies The French had extended to Canada the principles of tenure prevalent in Europe, modifying them only to the extent required by conditions in a new country

Under the French system all land remained the property of the king. The king made agreements with members of the nobility, granting to them large tracts of land, called seigniories, to be held in fief and administered by a seigneur with almost absolute authority The king required each seigneur to pay a nominal rent and to renew his allegiance annually. Furthermore, the king required the seigneur to take definite steps to settle the land allocated to him with a penalty of forfeiting his rights on failure to perform his obligations.

The seigneur provided grist mills, saw mills, the parish church, all necessary public works and military protection. He was truly lord and leader of his censitaires, protecting their interests in higher places where the peasants could scarcely expect to obtain hearing

The censitaire or peasant in his turn promised allegiance to the seigneur, tilled the soil and made contributions of labour as needed for the common welfare.

This system of land tenure produced a hierarchical society. At each of its levels, French Canadian society was a closely knit structure, with little or no political activity possible for the rank and file. The parish, usually co-terminus with the seigniory was a social rather than a geographical unit. In it there was a strong tradition of attachment to family and the home as well as to the village and the community.

The English had no desire to disturb these arrangements because they feared rightly that to do so would irrevocably antagonize the population and annoy the accepted leaders. Moreover, they knew that trouble was brewing in the older American colonies and they must avoid any additional problems in Canada. Therefore, the English made no attempt to change the system of land tenure. Indeed, after the Conquest the English followed the French practice of land grants.

The successful revolt of the British Colonies to the south against the authority of the Crown radically altered British imperial policy. The American revolution had not enlisted the sympathies of everyone in the colonies. Many preferred to retain their allegiance to England and made great personal sacrifices to do so. In justice, these loyalists had to receive compensation. It was not possible to welcome all loyalists back to the old country. The easiest solution was to grant them unsettled lands wherever they were available for colonization.

For this purpose the country north of Lake Ontario, and the region along the St. Lawrence River between Kingston and the mouth of the Ottawa River as well as large tracts in Nova Scotia were particularly suitable. Approximately thirty thousand loyalists received land grants in each of these areas.

The Crown made these grants under the same system of land tenure that applied in the British colonies, which was known as "free and common socage." The land was divided into townships, each approximately one hundred square miles in area. A fraction of the total area was reserved to the Crown with a similar portion set aside for the support of the Protestant Clergy. The settler who paid an agreed price for his land and carried out such improvements as might be specified in his "patent" became owner of the land. His only allegiance was to the Crown.

This form of landholding, as history has amply demonstrated, produced a society markedly different from that of French Canada. Although each proprietor depended to some extent upon the cooperation of his neighbours and the officers of the Crown, nevertheless he must rely largely on his own initiative to accomplish his aims. There was no legal binding or mutual interlocking

obligation. Hence, the township became a geographical rather than a social entity. Because there was no seigneur to safeguard his interests, each settler looked directly to the Crown for aid in major public undertakings The creation of "counties" was necessary for these larger undertakings and a representational system of central government took the place of the nobility. As a result the people developed a strong feeling for individual freedom and responsibility.

Under French rule it has been inferred that the wilderness area north and south of the St. Lawrence River below its junction with the Ottawa River was not used by the British authorities for meeting their obligations to the Loyalists. Apparently, Governor Haldimand cherished the hope that the French, who had proved their loyalty during the American Revolution, would settle in this region. Moreover, the Governor seemed fearful that the Loyalists might settle the areas bordering the American Republic and that in some future conflict they might not remain steadfastly loyal. Nevertheless the Loyalists exerted pressure to have this region opened to settlement.

A group of Loyalists, who, after the treaty in 1783 took refuge around the northernmost extension of Lake Champlain, known as Missisquoi Bay was particularly insistent about this matter. It is worthy of note that Vermont did not decide officially to join the New American nation until 1791 and for some time considered the idea of becoming a part of Canada. Many of the inhabitants of Vermont looked with envy at the fertile land in Canada which was far better suited to farming than parts of their own mountainous regions. After Vermont made its final decision to join the United States, some Loyalists were anxious to settle the vacant lands in Canada which many of them had explored.

In time this pressure from the stranded Loyalists coupled with the strong views of Lord Dorchester, the new governor, effected a change of policy in London. In 1791, authorization was given to survey all the land behind the back

4

limits of the seigniories already in existence on the shores of the St. Lawrence, the Ottawa, the Richelieu, the Yamaska and the Chaudiere Rivers and to sub-divide them into townships for settlement. Shortly after the surveying of the new townships the term "Eastern" Townships was used

The older townships of Ontario were certainly west of the new townships but the adjective "Western" was never applied to them. Nevertheless, some writers assumed that the adjective "Eastern" designated the newer townships from the older Ontario Townships. However, it must be noted that the townships along the Ottawa River and west of the Richelieu River are also west of the group presently known as the Eastern Townships and possibly the term "Eastern" was used to differentiate between these two groups.

The answer to this interesting speculation remains in doubt. A most careful search has not disclosed the origin of the term. Certainly by 1815 it was in general use because Bishop Charles James Stewart chose the title "A short view of the Present State of the Eastern Townships" for a publication.

The map on Plate 1 indicates the boundaries of the Eastern Townships. The western boundary is the "back lines" of the old seigniories along the Yamaska and Richelieu Rivers. The southern boundary separates the new American states from Canada, but the eastern end of this boundary was not established for some time after 1783 and a number of areas originally planned as townships eventually became part of New Hampshire and Maine. The Northern boundary follows the irregularities of the back lines of the seigniories along the St. Lawrence and the Chaudiere Rivers ending at the last fief a little south of the present town of St. George de Beauce. From this point on the Chaudiere to the American boundary townships were planned for both sides of the Chaudiere. However, the townships to the east of the Chaudiere are no longer considered a part of the Eastern Townships.

The Eastern Townships numbered about a hundred tracts of land, each approximately ten miles square. Each township was subdivided into lots of two hundred acres. Within the township one-seventh of the land was reserved for the Crown and one-seventh for the support of the Protestant Clergy. These reserves were scattered in such a way as to insure an equal distribution of the various types of land. The names assigned to the new Townships were derived almost entirely from existing place names in the British Isles.

The surveying of the Townships was a tremendous task covering an area approximately a hundred and twenty miles by a hundred miles. But in 1792 several surveying parties began work and by 1795 the task was almost completed although many of the original lines were subsequently changed.

Among the surveyors are the names of men, such as Simon Z. Watson, Theodore Depenciere, Jesse Pennoyer, Joseph Kilborn, James Rankin, James McDonell, Jeremiah McCarthy, among the draughtsmen are the names of Samuel Gale and John B. Duberger.

Royal instructions to Lord Dorchester in 1791 established the general terms under which settlers might legally acquire lands in the new townships. The provisions are worth quoting:

First. That the Crown Lands to be granted be parcel of a Township: If an Inland Township, of Ten Miles square, and if a Township on navigable Waters, Nine Miles in front and Twelve Miles in width, to be run out and marked by His Majesty's Surveyor or Deputy Surveyor General, or under His Sanction and Authority.

Second. That any such part of the Township be granted as shall remain, after a reservation of One-seventh Part thereof, for the support of a Protestant Clergy, and one other seventh part thereof for the future disposition of the Crown.

Third. That no Farm Lot shall be granted to any one person which shall contain more than Two Hundred Acres, yet the Governor, Lieutenant-Governor, or Person administering the Government, is allowed and permitted to grant to any Person or Persons such further Quantity of Land as they may desire, not exceeding One Thousand Acres over and above what may have been before granted them.

Fourth. That every Petitioner for Lands make it appear, that he or she is in a Condition to cultivate and improve the same, and shall besides taking the usual Oaths, subscribe a Declaration (before proper persons to be for that purpose appointed) of the Tenor of the Words following, viz. "I, A. B. do promise and declare that I will maintain and defend to the utmost of my Power the Authority of the King in His Parliament as the supreme Legislature of this Province."

Fifth. The Applications for Grants be made by Petition to the Governor, Lieutenant-Governor or Person administering the Government for the time being, and where it is advisable to grant the Prayer thereof a Warrant shall issue to the Proper Officer for a survey thereof, returnable within Six Months with a Plot annexed, and be followed with a Patent granting the same, if desired, in Free and Common Socage, upon the Terms and Conditions in the Royal Instruction expressed, and herein after suggested.

Sixth. That all grants reserve to the Crown all Coals, commonly called Sea Coals, and Mines of Gold, Silver, Copper, Tin, Iron and Lead; and each Patent contain a Clause for the Reservation of Timber for the Royal Navy of the Tenor following:

"And provided also, that no Part of the Tract or Parcel of Land hereby granted to the said   and his Heirs, be within any reservation heretofor made and marked for Us, Our Heirs and Successors by our Surveyor General of the Woods, or his lawful Deputy; in which Case, this our Grant for such Part of the Land hereby given and granted to the said   .   . and his Heirs for ever as aforesaid, and which shall upon a survey thereof being made, be found within any such Reservation, shall be null and void, anything herein contained to the contrary not withstanding."

Seventh. That the two sevenths reserved for the Crown's future disposition, and the Support

of a Protestant Clergy, be not severed Tracts each of One Seventh Part of the Township, but such Lots or Farms therein, as in the Surveyor General's Return of the Survey of the Township, shall be described as set apart for these purposes between the other Farms of which the said Township shall consist, to the Intent that the Lands so to be reserved, may be nearly of the like Value with an equal Quantity of the other parts to be granted out as afore-mentioned.

Eighth. That the respective Patentees are to take the Estates granted to them severally free of Quit rent and of any other Expenses, than such Fees as are or may be allowed to be demanded and received by the different Officers concerned in passing the Patent and recording the same, to be stated in a Table authorized and established by the Government and publickly fixed up in the several Offices of the Clerk of the Council, of the Surveyor-General, and of the Secretary of the Province.

Ninth. That every patent be entered upon the Record within Six months from the Date thereof, in the Secretary's or Register's Offices, and a Docket thereof in the Auditor's Office.

Tenth. Whenever it shall be thought adviseable to grant any given Quantity to one Person of one Thousand Acres or under, and the same cannot be found by reason of the said Reservations and prior Grants within the Township expressed, the same, or what shall be requisite to make up to such Person and Quantity advised, shall be located to him, in some other Township upon a new Petition for that purpose to be preserved.

GIVEN under my Hand and Seal at Arms at the Castle of Saint Lewis, in the City of Quebec, the Seventh Day of February, in the thirty-second year of His Majesty's Reign, and in the Year of Our Lord, one thousand seven hundred and ninety-two.

ALURED CLARKE.

By His Excellency's Council,
   HUGH FINLAY, Acting Secretary.

The following is a classification of petitioners

for waste lands of the Crown:

"A number of petitions were read from people who are praying for grants of the Waste Lands of the Crown, considering themselves to be entitled to His Majesty's Bounty. The Committee divided them into six classes.

"1st. Loyalists who have suffered from their attachment to the King's Government.

"2nd. Discharged Soldiers.

"3rd. Artificers discharged from the King's works after the war.

"4th. Sailors and others who served on the lakes etc.

"5th. Men who bore arms in the winter of the blockade.

"6th. Petitioners who have no particular pretensions to the King's Bounty, but who pray for Crown Lands as faithful subjects wishing to make immediate settlement on the lots that may be granted them."

The settlers had to bear the cost of surveying subdivisions and the cost of numerous trips to obtain official patents. Therefore, groups of prospective colonists applied for grants in the name of a leader who was a person capable of financing the venture. The first settlers who obtained a thousand or twelve hundred acres each were able to reimburse themselves by selling to others such portions of the land that they did not need.

Long delays between the petition and the issuance of a patent made it difficult to determine the real pioneers of the Eastern Townships. In many instances the eventual grantees had visited the lands they desired, and had even settled on them years before they received their title. As early as 1792 Gilbert Hyatt and Josiah Sawyer opened a wood road from Missisquoi Bay via Lake Memphramagog to Ascot. Nevertheless, Sawyer received his grant in Eaton only in 1800 and Hyatt received his grant in Ascot in 1803. Nicholas Austin settled in Bolton in 1793 and received his grant only in 1797.

The names of some of the pioneers and the districts in which they settled follow:

THOMAS SPENCER and ALEXANDER GRIGGS in Sutton Township.

ANDREW TEN EYCK in Dunham Township.

EBENEZER HOVEY in Hatley Township

EDMUND HEARD in Newport Township.

JOHN SAVAGE in Shefford Township

JOSIAH SAWYER in Eaton Township.

NICHOLAS AUSTIN in Bolton Township

ELEAZAR FITCH in Stanstead Township.

SILAS KNOWLTON and JOHN WHITNEY in Stukeley Township.

HUGH FINLAY in Stanbridge Township

MOSES COPP in Bolton Township

MOSES COWAN in Stoke Township

GILBERT HYATT in Ascot Township.

JOHNSON TAPLIN in Stanstead Township.

JOHN FRENCH in Eaton Township.

JOHN DONALDSON in Melbourne Township.

OZIAS CASWELL in Brompton Township.

JAMES RANKIN in Hereford Township.

NATHAN ANDREWS in Stanbridge Township.

JOHN BISHOP in Dudswell Township.

A summary of the adventures of three of these first settlers will illustrate the sort of life they encountered in their new homes.

Nicholas Austin came from Somersworth, N.H., and settled in Bolton, "of which township he was Patentee. In consequence of his firm allegiance to his Royal master during the troublous times in which he lived, he was persecuted by the government that came into power; and, leaving his family, he came to Canada, with intent to make his permanent residence here . . . Mr. Austin was warmly welcomed to Canada, of which country he had resolved on becoming a citizen . . . Fortunately, by address and the influence of his friends, he had saved his property from confiscation, but rather than live under a government he so thoroughly despised, he disposed of his beautiful estate at Somersworth . . . and prepared himself and his family for a new home in the wilds of Canada . . .

"On becoming joint proprietor of a township of land, Mr. Austin visited the premises, erected a log house and made a commencement; and, when he came in with his family, was accompanied by

7

a number of men hired for the purpose of clearing land They proceeded to chop and burn the timber on ninety-five acres, at which the smoke was so thick as for a time to obscure the sun, and great fear was felt lest their house should be burned, but by effort this calamity was prevented, and the land, thus, cleared and prepared immediately, that same season yielded one thousand bushels of corn.

"It is said that he came to Canada with an abundance of means; and, as it had been his ambition to become a large landed proprietor, his wealth was freely used in what he considered was for the good of the country, such as the construction of roads, bridges, mills, and in extensive surveys, &c.; but, whether his plans were not well matured before being put in practical operation, or whether there was a large infusion of the visionary element in his mental composition; it is apparent that from some cause, his anticipations were not in any good degree ever realized; and he had the grief and mortification of seeing his fortune wasting away before the untoward influences with which he was brought into contact. . .

"Mr. Austin was bred a Quaker; but in consequence of having married out of that society, he was looked upon as an alien, till by continued adhesion to the customs of the sect, he retrieved his standing and was forgiven, continuing to wear the Quaker garb and retaining their habits of speech till his death. We are not informed, however, whether he carried these manners into the drawing-rooms and to the tables where he was frequently admitted during his first visits to Quebec, though such was probably the case; as for the time he was an honored and welcome guest, and likely a privileged person. On one of these visits there a cannon was presented him by the Government, which in a very un-Quaker like manner he declared his purpose of mounting it on a high point of land running out from his estate into the lake, which small promontory he had named 'Point Gibraltar.' But for want of a road, and means of conveyance through the woods, the cannon was left in Quebec, and there remains to this day. He was unfortunate in his relations, his wife having suffered for years from a partial derangement of her mental faculties, which was probably induced by a (to her distasteful) change from a home of luxury and refinement, to the hardships and self-denials of life in the woods, involving, as it did, the loss of all moral and intellectual culture. . .

"They left their home in Somersworth when the snow was two and a half feet deep, with three yokes of oxen, one sled being loaded with hay and grain for the teams, the two others with the family, household goods and provisions. They had to camp out in the woods for nine nights after leaving the settlements in Vermont, before reaching their new home . . . at that time for many miles not a single settler could be found, not a tree cut, the land not even surveyed, and a "waste, howling wilderness" lay around for several day's journey; continuing so a number of years after Mr. Austin's first coming to the Magog. No mill or place where flour could be obtained was nearer than Danville, Vt., distant upward of forty miles."

"The corn they raised was at first pounded in a large wooden mortar in common use in the country wherever there were settlements at that period; and this continued until Mr. Austin purchased a small mill, which propelled by water from a brook near his residence, in a measure supplied the defficiency. . .

"Mr. Austin, senior, died in 1821, ruined in fortune and disappointed in hope. . . He had chosen his resting-place on the prominence he himself had named 'Point Gibraltar,' where he sleeps alone; the spot having been designated by a simple birch tree, which, however, was unfortunately cut down by mistake. . ."

Gilbert Hyatt, member of a large family from Arlington, Vt., has been mentioned as the leader in the settlement of Ascot, and hence the founder of the present city of Sherbrooke, first known as Hyatt's Mills. A few paragraphs quoted from documents addressed by him to Robert Shore

Milnes, then the Lieutenant Governor of Lower Canada, and his Council give a good idea of the difficulties encountered by those who risked their fortunes in attempting to provide leadership in the colonization of these newly created townships. He recites:

"That your Petitioner's Father Voluntarily took up arms in support of the Crown and joined General Burgoyne's army during the Campaign of 1777 — Upon his return home, being greatly persecuted by the Americans, for his loyalty, he found means to take refuge in this province with his wife, seven sons and three daughters, in the year 1780. That your petitioner also bore arms during the remainder of the American contest in the Regiment of Loyal Americans, under the command of Major Jessup, until the reduction of 1783 — and has never received any part of His Majesty's Bounty in lands for said services.

That your Petitioner obtained a Warrant of Survey for the Township of Ascot in 1792, the outlines of which were immediately run; when the Petitioner and his Associates commenced a settlement therein, and caused the same to be accurately surveyed and subdivided in 1794.

That your Petitioner was the first person who attempted to settle the Wild Lands of the Crown in the said County of Bedford, and opened a road for about sixty miles from any inhabitants to the said Township, thereby enhancing the value of the Crown and Clergy reserves and encouraging others by his example and perseverance to do the like.

That your Excellency's Petitioner has at all times endeavoured to conform himself (according to the best of his judgment) to the rules and regulations prescribed, so soon as they came to his knowledge and prosecuted the settlement of the Township aforesaid with the greater Spirit and Zeal, from a presumption that he was fulfilling the wishes of the Government. But has been greatly distressed in mind since he has understood that he acted prematurely and had done wrong — Nevertheless consoled in some measure by a strong conviction of the rectitude of his intentions, while labouring under the impression that he was performing a work acceptable in the eyes of Government, and the consciousness of his loyalty and attachment to the British Crown and Constitution, (which he conceives cannot be questioned from the circumstances above related) he is induced to hope and emboldened to beseech your Excellency, that no unfavourable construction may be put upon his having taken possession without a better title than a Warrant of Survey That it may be considered merely as an error of judgment, to which much more enlightened men than himself are liable, and that no harsh interpretation thereof be suffered to operate against his pretentions to a grant of the said Township of Ascot.

That the Petitioner and his associates have been at great trouble, anxiety and expense in establishing forty actual settlers, who, together with their families, number one hundred and two souls; that their disbursements collectively, including the cost of mills, dwelling houses, barns and other buildings, with real improvements at a moderate computation, exceeds the sum of four thousand pounds currency, as appears by a statement thereof upon oath and which can be proved by the testimony of persons here present.

That this is the fifth journey that your Excellency's Petitioner, to his great cost and waste of time, has made to Quebec to prosecute this business; and should he now fail of obtaining a grant of the whole of the said Township, he must be a considerable sufferer, thereby, as it will be impossible for him — otherwise to fulfill the engagement he has entered into with his associates and others. . ."

It would be pleasant to be able to record that Hyatt received satisfaction. He did not. The above was dated 24 January, 1800; in February, 1801 he protests the decision of "Your Excellency in Council on his case," that if this decision stands, he will be ruined. Unhappily, he eventually was ruined, and the best of his holdings seized by the sheriff to satisfy his creditors.

It is scarcely surprising that Samuel Gale of

9

Farnham who, as an employee of the Surveyor General's office, was in a position to know "these delays had been occasioned in order that other persons might put in claims for grants of the lands after improvements had been made and the land more valuable." He also claimed that more than two years passed after the promulgation of the Royal instructions and warrants for surveys before any Commissioners for administrating the necessary oaths had been appointed.

Mrs. Day supplies an account of another Township leader, John Bishop, to whose heirs one fourth of Dudswell was granted in 1805. "John Bishop, who had enlisted in the American revolutionary army, was taken prisoner by the British, and as such carried to Quebec. It appears that during this lengthened captivity, his uniform good conduct and obliging behaviour, so far won upon the good will of those in charge of the prison, that as a mark of approbation and particular favor, he was granted access to books, and was likewise assisted in the study of mathematics for which he had a decided taste. Naturally gifted with quick perceptions and a retentive memory, and being withal of an observant and inquiring nature, he readily saw that in patiently resigning himself to the necessities of his situation, and improving his powers and opportunities to the utmost of his ability, he was fitting himself to meet any emergency that might arise.

"By these means he acquired a knowledge of the science of surveying, which, after his return home, was turned to practical account. He followed this profession several years in Vermont, during which time he married and settled in life, but at length decided on a removal to Canada.

"Having formed valuable acquaintances with parties in Quebec during his compulsory sojourn in that city, he visited it again, this time voluntarily, and was highly favored in meeting with friends who were able and willing to forward his wishes and plans, he therefore took the preliminary steps toward obtaining for himself and associates the grant of a township of land. Next he visited the tract designated, made some

necessary preparation for a removal thither, and returned to Vermont. In October, 1800, he brought his wife and seven children — the latter all under fifteen years of age — to the new home provided for them in the wilderness of Dudswell...

"Business connected with the settlement of which he was head and founder, required Mr. Bishop to be frequently from home; during which journeys he was often a sufferer from fatigue and exposure. On one of them made in the month of March, he was taken sick and lay ill at the house of a friend about 14 miles from home, till the following June, when, anxious as he said, to reach his home to die, he was carefully conveyed to the River St. Francis, and brought in an Indian bark canoe to within a short distance of the house to which he was with difficulty removed, and from which he never again ventured, though he lived till August.

". . . Much of Mr. Bishop's success in obtaining the required number of associates, had been owing to his personal popularity as a man of energy, ability, and integrity — qualities that gave him great influence. Unfortunately his death took place at a time when the stability of the settlement was by no means assured. . .

"The conditions by which the charter of the Township was to be obtained, had not to any great extent been complied with, yet several families had moved on to the premises in good faith, and many others had pledged themselves to do the same. . .

"In this doubtful state of the business, Naphali Bishop, a brother of the deceased, came forward to assume charge of his late relative's affairs; and after much embarrassment and delay, succeeded in obtaining a grant of one quarter of the township, by which manner titles to the lands that had been settled upon, were confirmed to the occupants."

For the new settlers, potato whiskey and "pot" and "pearl" ash seem to have been the main source of cash income, because other products of the soil were too bulky for profitable shipment to available markets. "Pot" and "pearl" ash were merely the concentrates of the lye obtained as a by-product from clearing the land of hard wood forests Their production continued for a century. The techniques of this process are well described in a pamphlet issued in 1871 to encourage French Canadians to settle in the Eastern Townships The writer of this pamphlet, the Rev. J B. Chartier, explains that the settler must first clear the underbrush from the forest leaving only the larger trees to be felled during the winter months. In cutting these down, he explains, one takes care to make them fall parallel, and not criss-cross, which is a nuisance when the time comes to pile them. Once felled, the trees are cut into logs between 10 and 20 feet long, according to the thickness of the trunks and also according to the strength of the bullocks used to pile them. They are at once stripped of their branches, which are piled and burned. Then the logs themselves are piled, and here a good team of oxen is almost indispensable. Piles of small soft woods can be made by a man working with his own arms, but even in this case nothing can take the place of a good yoke of oxen... The settler chooses a slightly elevated spot and begins by having his bullocks drag seven or eight logs there, placing them side by side. Then, with levers, he puts another row on top of the first, and so forth, until he reaches the top of the pyramid. The number of such piles per acre will naturally depend on the thickness of the forest; six or seven is the average. The moment a pile is finished, one sets it on fire. Hard woods burn in any season; there is no need of waiting until they dry out. And often the burning is done in the midst of winter, with snow all around. Once the wood is consumed, the ashes from each pile are carefully gathered and placed in a sheltered place, where they cannot be damaged by rain... Later the ash is steeped in tubs or large troughs with an opening at one end, and the resultant lye is boiled, exactly like maple sap. Once it has been reduced, it becomes potash. This salt brings in about $2.50 per 100 pounds It takes 22 to 24 bushels of ash to make a hundred pounds of salt, and an acre of good

hardwood will yield 75 to 80 bushels of ash Since the cost of clearing an acre had remained about $10 00 from the time of the first settlements, and the price of "pot" or "pearl" had once been as high as $6 00 per cwt , a cash profit resulted from the clearing process alone

Once the settlements had attained a certain size, the best cash income was certainly whiskey The size of this trade can be realized from the fact that at one time Stanstead Plain had no less than twenty-six distilleries, each reported to produce annually an average of three thousand gallons The settlers sent the larger part of this to the Montreal market although early writers indicate that the settlers consumed far too much of it at home. As communications improved, the settlers took other products to market. For instance, after the army built the Craig's Road to Quebec in 1811 the settlers sent meat to the Quebec market

Although arduous conditions prevailed, life was tolerable and immigration continued at an encouraging pace for about two decades Early in the 19th century the population of each of the following communities was approximately — Stanstead 3000, Dunham 2000, Barnston, Hatley and Stanbridge 1500, Bolton, Brome and Compton 1000. The populations of a few more communities approached the thousand mark.

The war of 1812 and the opening of the American west substantially reduced the rate of English immigration to the Eastern Townships. Furthermore, some settlers left the Eastern Townships. At the same time, over-population became a problem in the old French Canadian communities. Yet, the Townships attracted very few of the young French Canadians. The Catholic clergy were indifferent to French Canadian settlement in the Eastern Townships because of the land reserves assigned to the Crown and the Protestant clergy. In his Topographical Dictionary (1832) Bouchette constantly adverts to this French unwillingness to settle in the Townships. Thus, he says of the parish of St. Jean Baptiste on the Island of Orleans

"The old farms are too much divided and the number of small emplacements on barren soils are constantly increasing; and their occupants carry on trades without a knowledge of scarcely the first elements; they bring up families of wretched beings destined to increase the number of mendicants " Yet, "Not a single parishoner has migrated to the Townships, for the mode of concession there practiced is not agreeable to them."

The practice of granting large tracts of land in the Eastern Townships to influential individuals was instituted for the purpose of attracting settlers Nevertheless, it proved to be a failure because these persons acquired their holdings in the hope of making a profit and they held out for prices which were beyond the means of many prospective settlers. Lord Durham was scandalized to learn in 1838 that as few as one hundred and five owners held one million and five hundred thousand acres of land. Among the recipients of these large grants were: Robert Shore Milnes, the Lieutenant-Governor who acquired 60,000 acres, George Hamilton, an early benefactor of Bishop's College received 8,000 acres in Leeds; Joseph Frobisher in Ireland, William McGillivray in Inverness and Simon McTavish, the famous fur-trader in Chester.

The Canada Land Company was organized in Ontario in 1824 to correct a somewhat similar situation. Its charter of 1826 was granted for the purpose of bringing colonists to the Upper Canada Townships and disposing of the Crown and Clergy Reserves. The astute management of John Galt, a brilliant Scot made this enterprise flourish. The success of this enterprise suggested that a similar company might be 'as successful in encouraging immigration to Lower Canada. For this purpose the British American Land Company was formed and agreed to purchase 251,000 acres of Crown Reserves and other Crown Lands in the counties of Shefford, Stanstead and Sherbrooke. In addition, the Company purchased 596,000 acres in undeveloped parts of the St. Francis Territory, then a part of the County of Sherbrooke, and now largely in the County of Compton. The acreage was soon increased to a million and a quarter. The Company employed Arthur C. Webster as manager and chose Sherbrooke as the Canadian Headquarters. It launched an energetic campaign to encourage immigration from the old countries.

Competition between the Canada Land Company and the British American Land Company became very keen. The agents of the British American Land Company, posted in Quebec and Montreal, tried to deflect prospective settlers from Upper to Lower Canada. The Company established easy terms for the colonists and requested as little as twenty per cent of the purchase price in cash with the balance due within three years. The company supplied provisions for the first winter. It offered help with the clearing of the land and with the building of a home.

At first this policy appeared to be successful as exemplified by the settlement at Victoria in the Township of Bury which attracted about 300 families. By 1836 settlers had purchased 33,000 acres of the company's land. Yet, two years later, only one of the families remained at Victoria. The exodus may have been caused by the Rebellion of 1837. But, it is more likely that the Company had promised too much and the settlers found that life in the new settlement was far more rigorous and less profitable than they had anticipated.

Alexander Tilloch Galt played a large part in solving the aforementioned problems of the British American Land Company and in assuring its later success. Alexander Tilloch Galt came to Sherbrooke in 1835 at the age of eighteen to serve as a clerk in the new Company. He was the son of John Galt, a founder of both the Canada Land Company and the British American Land Company. He seems to have won the respect of his superiors and in 1840 the Company gave him the task of collecting money owed by settlers, and of recommending a more practical policy.

Galt's report in 1842 to the directors in London included the following recommendations: the cancellation of debts of many of the destitute settlers, the granting of greater discretion to the Company commissioner; greater efforts to attract French Canadians; the attraction of industry to Sherbrooke where abundant water power existed, the favouring of Canadian and American settlers familiar with the region; a more careful selection of prospective immigrants; the avoidance of heavy burdens on the settlers during their first years and the opportunity for the settlers to pay their debts in services.

The directors endorsed Galt's report and made him secretary of the Company with a full mandate to carry out his recommendations. By 1851, Galt was able to announce that the Company was in good financial condition with a cash surplus of 100,000 pounds.

The foundation of the French Canadian Colonization Society in 1847, which gave added stimulus to French settlement, and the building of the St Lawrence and Atlantic Railroad, which alleviated the problems of transportation in the Townships, were important factors in achieving the goals of the British American Land Company.

Galt resigned his post with the Company in 1855 to enter the service of the Government of Canada and later became a father of Confederation. R. W Heneker succeeded him in the British American Land Company. The Company continued to operate for more than a century. It surrendered its charter in 1947.

The authors hope that this brief summary of historical facts will be an interesting supplement to the pictorial record of prints which have been collected for this book.

Plate 3 —— PANORAMIC VIEW OF SHERBROOKE FROM
THE EAST SIDE OF THE RIVER ST. FRANCIS, 1834

*The village of Sherbrooke occupies an elevated situation on
both banks of the river Magog, at the Forks of St. Francis. It
contains about 75 houses, and its settlements are connected
by a tolerable good bridge, near which are Mr. Goodhue's
mills. The churches and the greater part of the village
are in Orford, but the old court-house and the gaol are on the
Ascott side of the river. The population is about 350.
It is the seat of the jurisdiction of the inferior district
of St. Francis, and is a place of more general resort than any
of the villages in the neighbouring townships. it is, as it were,
the emporium of the township trade, and the place of
transit through which the chief part of the township
commodities are conveyed to the St. Lawrence. These
commodities are, chiefly, pot and pearl-ashes, horses,
horned cattle, and some sheep.*

JOS. BOUCHETTE, 1831

Plate 2   LENNOXVILLE DISTRICT OF
ST FRANCIS, L.C., IN 1832

Lennoxville, about three miles south of Sherbrooke, is
situated in lot 10, 5th range, on a rising ground on the south
side of a branch of the St Francis It contains about
20 houses, and its population is about 120 The church,
seated on a rising ground south of the road, is built of larger
size than is necessary for the extent or population of
the parish The houses of this village are scattered along the
public road leading to Compton and other townships
near the province line

JOS BOUCHETTE, 1831

PANORAMIC VIEW OF SHERBROOKE, FROM THE EAST SIDE
IN THE DISTRICT OF ST. FRANCIS, PROVINCE OF LOWER CANADA,—CANADA

From an Original Sketch.

Plate 4 — KILBORN'S MILLS, STANSTEAD, LR. CANADA
& THE UNITED STATES SETTLEMENTS, 1836

In 1821, Mr Charles Kilborn was proprietor of lots
in the 8th and 9th ranges, containing together 400 acres,
of which he had cleared about 100, the cost of clearing and
inclosing which was about £ 3 per acre He then possessed
upwards of 200 head of cattle, including sheep, and
had erected on his farm 3 dwelling-houses, two barns,
a grist-mill, a saw-mill, a fulling-mill, a carding-machine,
and other buildings, which cost him upwards of £ 1,500
but which he valued in 1821 at only about £ 750   There were
many persons whose farms were more improved, who had
a greater number of cattle, and whose buildings were
far more valuable than Mr. Kilborn's. —— This T. is well
watered by rivers and lakes — The Village of Stanstead
is built near the province line and consists of 23 houses and
200 souls, the houses are in general neat and substantial;
many of them two stories high and several are built with
brick The style of building is very different here and
throughout the township to what is practised in the
seignorial settlements of the province, and borders considerably,
if not absolutely, to the American style as practised in the
adjoining state of Vermont.

JOS. BOUCHETTE, 1831

PLATE 4

KINGDOMS HILL, STANSTEAD & THE UNITED STATES SEEN BEYOND

From "BRITISH AMERICAN LAND COMPANY VIEWS IN LOWER CANADA," 1836 — Drawn by Col. Joseph Bouchette   Reprinted 1961

*Resuming the subject of the eastern townships, it will be
found that, in the tract of country known by that name,
98 whole townships and parts of townships have been
at different times laid out and subdivided by actual survey
and that ten more remain to be admeasured and erected by
letters patent, to complete the internal division of the tract.
Very few, if any, of the townships thus surveyed, can be said
to be wholly destitute of settlers, although by far the greater
number present but unconnected and partial settlements
thinly scattered over the country. The townships most
settled are Ascot, Eaton, Compton, Hatley, Stanstead,
Barnston, Barford, Potton, Sutton, Dunham, Stanbridge,
Farnham, Brome, Bolton, Orford, Stukeley, and Shefford,
which form the mass of townships on the frontier of the
province, about Lake Memphramagog and the forks
of the St. Francis.*

Jos. Bouchette, 1832

PLATE 5

VIEW ON THE LITTLE LEEUWTER

From "BRITISH AMERICAN LAND COMPANY VIEWS IN LOWER CANADA," 1846 — *Drawn by Col. Joseph Bouchette or R.S.M. Bouchette*　　　*Reprinted 1952*

Plate 6 — SHERBROOKE, EASTERN TOWNSHIPS, 1836

The town of Sherbrooke contains about 50 dwelling houses, it occupies a high position on both banks of the River Magog, at the forks of the St Francis, and its settlements are connected by a bridge, the old court-house and jail are on the Ascot side. As the seat of jurisdiction of the district of St. Francis, it is a place of general resort; besides being, as it were, the emporium of the township trade, or rather (as the head of the present navigation of the St Francis), the place of transit through which the chief part of the township produce is conveyed to the market towns, or elsewhere The chief articles of trade are grain, pot and pearl ashes, and likewise horses, horned cattle, sheep, and other livestock

JOS. BOUCHETTE, 1832

PLATE 6

LOWER CANADA
PRINCIPAL STATION OF THE BRITISH AMERICAN LAND COMPANY

From "BRITISH AMERICAN LAND COMPANY VIEWS IN LOWER CANADA," 1836 — *Drawn by Col. Joseph Bouchette or R.S.M. Bouchette*   *Reprinted 1962*

Plate 7 — WOOLLEN FACTORY, SHERBROOKE, IN THE
EASTERN TOWNSHIPS, LOWER CANADA, 1836

*The town of Sherbrooke, where the British American
Land Company's principal establishment is fixed, is the
capital of the eastern townships . . . It contains several
well built houses, mostly of brick, three places of worship, viz.,
Episcopalian, Dissenting, and Roman Catholic, the Court-
House and Gaol of the District, the County Register
Office; a classical academy, a commodious inn, and
a printing office, at which a weekly newspaper, "The
Sherbrooke Gazette," is published. Grist and Saw Mills,
belonging to the Company, as also a woollen factory, have
been for some time in operation, the latter offers to an
intelligent and active manufacture, with small capital,
a very favourable opening for its investment, and the
exertion of his energies in the making of course strong
articles similar to some manufactured in Yorkshire and
Westmoreland. The water power is applicable to mills
and machinery to almost any extent*

R. MONTGOMERY MARTIN, 1838

PLATE 7

From "BRITISH AMERICAN LAND COMPANY VIEWS IN LOWER CANADA," 1836 — *Drawn by Col Joseph Bouchette or R S M Bouchette*   *Reprinted 1962*

Plate 9 — Lake Memphremagog, 1839 · 1842

Memphramagog, lake, is in the co of Stanstead, stretching
its southern extremity into the state of Vermont It
separates the townships of Stanstead and Hatley from
those of Potton and Bolton It is of a semicircular shape,
20 miles long and very narrow It empties itself into the
R. St Francis by means of the R Magog, which runs
through Lake Scaswannepus — In this lake are several
kinds of fish, particularly salmon-trout

Jos Bouchette, 1831

PLATE 9

Plate 10 — VIEW ACROSS THE BOUNDARY LINE,
1839 - 1842

*Stanstead village is the next in the scale of consequence,
although in point of neatness it takes precedence of
Sherbrooke The buildings are generally more regular and
tasty, many of them, two stories high, and several are
built of brick The style of buildings throughout the
townships is very different from that followed in the
French settlements of the province, and borders considerably,
if it is not absolutely similar, to the American Style, in the
adjoining state of Vermont ... The domestic cleanliness
usually to be met in the houses of the inhabitants is such
as to characterise them for that virtue, whilst domestic
manufacturers of every description, introduced in the
Country, such as homespun clothes and linens, drapes &c.,
are evidence of their industry some of the cloths and linens
are of a tissue and texture, not much inferior to the common
description of imported British cloths and Irish linens.*

JOS. BOUCHETTE, 1832

PLATE 10

Rock amid the bounding line

From "CANADIAN SCENERY," 1840-1842, by W H Bartlett   Reprinted 1962

Plate 11 —— LAKE MASSAWHIPPY, 1839 - 1842

*Lake Tomifobi or Massawippi lies in the Township of
Hatley, length about 9 miles, average width 1-1/2 miles.
The scenery about this lake is quite equal to any in this
section. In this Lake is found a greater variety of fish than in
any lake in the Eastern Townships*

W. S. HUNTER, JR., 1860

PLATE 11

From "CANADIAN SCENERY," 1839-1842, by W H Bartlett

Reprinted 1962

Plate 12 ------ LAKE BENEATH THE OWLS HEAD
MOUNTAIN, 1839 · 1842

*Owl's Head is estimated to be 2500 feet above the level of
Lake Memphremagog, and is situated on the western shore,
about the centre of the Lake Many others of less altitude
are scattered throughout the Eastern Townships.*

W S HUNTER, JR., 1860

PLATE 12

From "CANADIAN SCENERY," 1839-1842, by W. H. Bartlett   Reprinted 1967

Plate 13 — JUNCTION OF THE ST. FRANCIS AND
MAGOG RIVERS, 1839 - 1842

*The confluence of the united waters of the rivers Massiwippi,
Coaticook, and Salmon River, with the R. St. Francis,
near Lennoxville, is called the Upper Locks, and the junction
of the R. Magog with the St Francis at Sherbrooke Village
is called the Lower Locks A little below Hyatt's Mills
there is a very singular high rock in the river, on the
pinnacle of which stands one solitary pine-tree of large
dimensions, the rock and the tree form an object
extraordinarily unique.*

JOS. BOUCHETTE, 1831

PLATE 13

From "CANADIAN SCENERY," 1839-1842, by W H Bartlett

Reprinted 1962

Plate 14 — BRIDGE AT SHERBROOKE, 1839 - 1842

Magog River, in the Cos of Stanstead and Sherbrooke,
rises in Lake Memphramagog, from the N E extremity of
which it issues, and running through Lake Scaswaninepus
forms the boundary line between Ascot and Orford, and
falls into the River St Francis at the village of Sherbrooke,
where it constitutes the Forks of Ascot commonly called
the Lower Locks — It runs about 14 miles from the
Lake Scaswaninepus

JOS BOUCHETTE, 1831

PLATE 14

From "CANADIAN SCENERY, 1839-1842, by W. H Bartlett   Reprinted 1962

Plate 15 — ORFORD MOUNTAIN, 1839 - 1842

Orford Mountain, the highest in the Townships, situated near the northern extremity of Lake Memphremagog, has an elevation of about 4,500 feet above the St Lawrence From its summit may be seen in one panoramic view eighteen lakes, all emptying themselves into the Yamaska and the Richelieu on the one hand, and the St Francis on the other.

W. S HUNTER, JR , 1860

PLATE 1

Plate 16 —— GEORGEVILLE, 1839 - 1842

Earlier known as Copp's Ferry, and named after
Cap't Moses Copp, first settler in the vicinity in 1797
Cap't Copp ran the first boat on the lake. The name was
changed to Georgeville in 1822 after George, first male
born there and the son of Moses Copp.
The first steam boat on the lake was built there by
Geo. W Fogg and Col. Cross — the "Mountain Maid".
Post-Office was established in 1827, one of the earliest in
the Eastern Townships

PLATE 16

From "CANADIAN SCENERY," 1839-1842, by W. H. Bartlett

Reprinted 1962

Plate 17 — OUTLET OF LAKE MEMPHREMAGOG,
1839 - 1842

A thriving village romantically situated at the
Outlet of Lake Memphremagog, in the township of
Magog, county of Stanstead. It possesses a considerable
extent of water power, which is made use of for various
manufacturing purposes. In the summer season a steamer
runs to and from Newport, Vt., daily; fare $1.00 There
are two churches in the village, Roman Catholic, and
Union, a model and district school, two saw mills,
one grist mill, cloth dressing and carding mill.

EASTERN TOWNSHIPS GAZETTEER, 1867

PLATE 17

Falls of the Montmorency

Plate 18 —— MILLS AT SHERBROOKE, ON THE
RIVER MAGOG, 1839 - 1842

Jos Bouchette in 1831 lists the following Mills
in operation in Ascott Township in the county of Sherbrooke·

Corn Mills........	2
Saw Mills........	3
Potasheries	2
Pearlasheries . . .	2
Tanneries	1

He also states that at the foot of the Great Falls are
Hyatt's Mills belonging to Gilbert Hyatt to whom with
several associates the township was originally granted. The
distillation of whiskey from potatoes was also a source
of great profit. He mentions Mr. Goodhue's Mills. It is
quite conceivable that by 1839 a few more mills were
established. The British American Land Company had set
up a woollen mill

PLATE 18

From "CANADIAN SCENERY," 1839-1842, by W. H. Bartlett

Reprinted 1962

Plate 19 — VIEW OVER LAKE MEMPHREMAGOG,
1839 · 1842

Lake Memphremagog is about 30 miles long, by a breadth
of generally about 2 miles, but in some parts of the Lake
three or more It lies in a semi-circular form, partly among
the mountains, and partly in the valley beyond, which
obliquely crosses the northern portion, stretching its southern
extremity into the State of Vermont, about one-third of
the Lake belonging to the United States

W. S. HUNTER, JR , 1860

PLATE 19

Plate 20 — DAVIS CLEARING, 1839-1842

*No information whatsoever has been located on this print
and although it does have the appearance of Lake
Memphremagog or Massawippi and is marked
"Eastern Townships" it could be elsewhere in Canada.
The name has not been located in any Historical or
Geographical reference works.*

PLATE 20

From "CANADIAN SCENERY," 1839-1842, *by* W H Bartlett

Reprinted 1962

Plate 21 — Pass of Bolton, Eastern Townships,
1839 - 1842

*Bolton Pass discovered by Lester Ball who reported to
Col P H. Knowlton that it was a favorable place
to construct a road.*

E. M. Taylor, 1908

PLATE 21

From "CANADIAN SCENERY," 1839-1842, by W. H. Bartlett   Reprinted 1961

Plate 22 — A Lake Farm on the Frontier,
1839-1842

*Although no designation on the print indicates this is
the Eastern Townships, the appearance in general indicates
that it fits into this "Frontier" scenery more than other
localities painted by Bartlett.*

PLATE 22

A Lake Scene on the Ottawa

From "CANADIAN SCENERY," 1839-1842, by W. H. Bartlett

Reprinted 1962

PLATE 23

From "CANADIAN SCENERY," 1839-1842, by W. H. Bartlett

Reprinted 1967

Plate 24 — THE OWLS HEAD, 1839 - 1842

Owl's Head is estimated to be 2500 feet above the level of Lake Memphremagog, and is situated on the western shore, about the centre of the Lake Many others of less altitude are scattered throughout the Eastern Townships

W. S. HUNTER, JR , 1860

PLATE 24

From "CANADIAN SCENERY," 1839-1842, by W H Bartlett

Reprinted 1962

Plate 25 — A Settler's Hut on the Frontier,
1839-1842

*Although no designation on the print indicates this is
the Eastern Townships, the appearance in general indicates
that it fits into this "Frontier" scenery more than other
localities painted by Bartlett*

PLATE 25

From "CANADIAN SCENERY," 1839-1842, by W H Bartlett

Reprinted 1962

Plate 26 — SCENE ON THE RIVER ST FRANCIS
NEAR SHERBROOKE, 1839-1842

*The St Francis River source is Lake St. Francis in the
County of Frontenac about 60 miles north-east of Sherbrooke,
and discharges by a narrow channel into Aylmer Lake,
which is drained by the St. Francis River, which flows
south-west, and then turning sharply to the north-west at
Lennoxville, flows into the St. Lawrence, on its right bank
at Lake St Peter.*

PLATE 26

From "CANADIAN SCENERY," 1839-1842, by W. H. Bartlett

Reprinted 1962

Plate 27 — COPP'S FERRY, 1839 - 1842

Copp's Ferry —— Named after Capt. Moses Copp from Massachusetts who came to Canada in 1796 and settled at "Copp's Ferry" in 1797. He built the first boat on Lake Memephremagog The name Copp's Ferry was changed to Georgeville in 1822

PLATE 27

From "CANADIAN SCENERY," 1839-1842, by W. H. Bartlett

Reprinted 1962

Stanstead Plain is situated in the County of Stanstead and near the Frontier Line It is incorporated as a municipality, and has a population of about 1000 It is the business-centre of one of the most wealthy agricultural counties in the Eastern Townships. It is beautifully situated on a plain, commanding a great range of Alpine scenery extending as far as the eye can reach, southerly, along the Green Mountains of Vermont and their continuation into Canada, along the western shore of the beautiful and picturesque Lake Memphremagog, till they are lost in northern distance.

W. S Hunter, Jr., 1860

PLATE 28

From "CANADIAN SCENERY," 1839-1842, by W. H Bartlett

Reprinted 1962

Plate 29 — BISHOP'S COLLEGE, LENNOXVILLE, 1846

Bishop's College was so named because it owed its origin
to the efforts of Bishop Mountain. The college first opened
its doors for the term of 1845 - 1846 This lithograph
is the earliest known picture of the college.

PLATE 29

BISHOP'S MILLE, LENNOXVILLE

From "SONGS OF THE WILDERNESS," by George J. Mountain, D.D. — Drawn by T. Picken, Lithographed by Day & Haghe. 1846   Reprinted 1982

Plate 30 — The Bridge at the Outlet, 1836-1842 (Printed c. 1860)

Copied from W. H. Bartlet's "Outlet of Lake Memphremagog"

See description for Plate 17.

PLATE 5

THE BRIDGE AT THE OUTLET

Lithographed by Currier & Ives, c. 1M

Plate 31 — LAKE MEMPHREMAGOG (OWL'S HEAD), 1839-1842 (Printed c. 1860)

Copied from W. H. Bartlett's "Owl's Head" Lake Memphremagog
See description for Plate 24

PLATE 31

Reproduced 1/2

Lithographed by Currier & Ives, c 1800

Plate 32 — LAKE MEMPHRAMAGOG, C. E., 1860

Mount Pleasant, the residence of M. W. Copp, Esq., whence this view was taken, is situated one mile in a northerly direction from the village of Magog, at the northern extremity of the lake. From this point we see but half of the lake, but the view conveys a clear idea of its scenery, its winding wooded shores, shooting into promotories or withdrawing into lovely bays. The majestic mountains which stretch along its western shore, prominent among which is "Owl's Head," with its conical and picturesque outline, give a truly Alpine character to the scene. The eastern shore of the lake, with its gentle slopes and cultivated farms, presents a pleasing contrast to the western one.

W. S. HUNTER, JR., 1860

PLATE 32

LAKE MEMPHREMAGOG, C. E.

Looking South from the residence of M. W. Copp, Esq. Mt Pleasant, W. 1862.

Plate 33 — View on the St. Francis near Sherbrooke, 1860

This view is taken from East Sherbrooke at a point near the bridge crossing the St. Francis The highland in the background is formed by the winding of the river at this point The banks are here gently sloping for a few feet, until they reach the meadow-land, traversing which we soon attain the hills beyond. On the left, the shores are skirted by beautiful elms, overhanging the river-side.

W. S. Hunter, Jr., 1860

PLATE 33

VIEW ON THE ST FRANCIS NEAR SHERBROOKE

Plate 34 — VIEW FROM THE ARTIST'S RESIDENCE, 1860

The artist has taken the liberty of giving a view from his own residence, considering it as he does one of much beauty. It embraces the range of mountains west of Lake Memphremagog, Owl's-Head occupying the centre of the picture, with a glimpse of the lake at the left. A tract of highly cultivated country occupies the space between the back and fore ground The road in view is one leading from Stanstead Plain to Rock Island

W. S. HUNTER, JR., 1860

PLATE 34

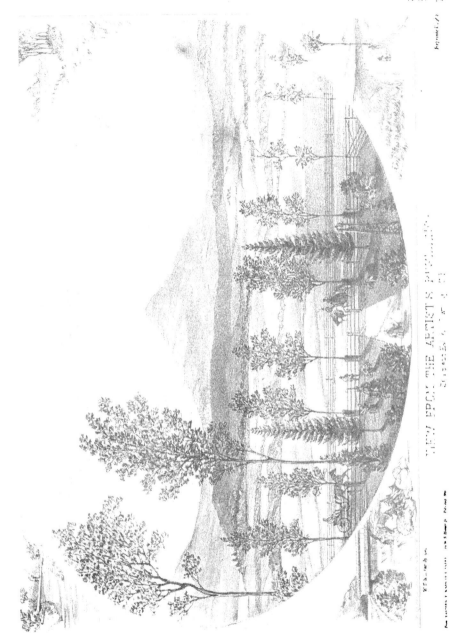

VIEW FROM THE ARTIST'S BEDROOM.

Plate 35 — LAKE MASSAWIPPI, 1860

This view is taken from the road leading to East Hatley, from Massawippi Village. From this point, nearly the whole extent of the lake is opened up to view; mirror-like reflecting the mountains which bound the opposite shore. Its shores are richly wooded, and indented by winding bays and points jutting into the lake In the middle distance and to the right of the picture, is Blackberry Mountain

W. S. HUNTER, JR., 1860

PLATE 35

LAKE VIEW, OREGON.

Plate 36 — Falls on the Coaticook River, 1860

These Falls may be reached by leaving the highway between the Villages of Compton and Coaticook, at a point of the road distant about a mile from the latter village. These romantic falls extend a mile or more. Our view is taken from the interior of the chasm, looking down the river. Here the spectator is surrounded on all sides with rocks of great height, fringed with tangled masses of shrubs and trees, nourished by the constant spray ascending from the boiling waters beneath.

W. S. HUNTER, JR., 1860

PLATE 36

Plate 37 — VIEW OF OWL'S HEAD FROM SUGAR LOAF MOUNTAIN
LOOKING SOUTH, 1860

Gazing from some of the heights or promontories which here surround us, one feels
"raptured and amazed." Now we behold Owl's-Head, where the grey rocks dip down into
unfathomable water; now deep, retreating bays, then bold and rugged shores which have
been washed for ages by the waters of Lake Memphremagog.

Owl's-Head, the highest mountain which rises from the shores of the lake, is situated
on the western side near the centre of the lake. Its height is 2500 feet from the surface
of the lake. In the extreme southern distance may be seen Willoughby Notch, and
to the left of the illustration a portion of the highly cultivated Township of Stanstead,
to the south, the lake, with its islands studding its mirrored surface.

W. S. HUNTER, JR., 1860

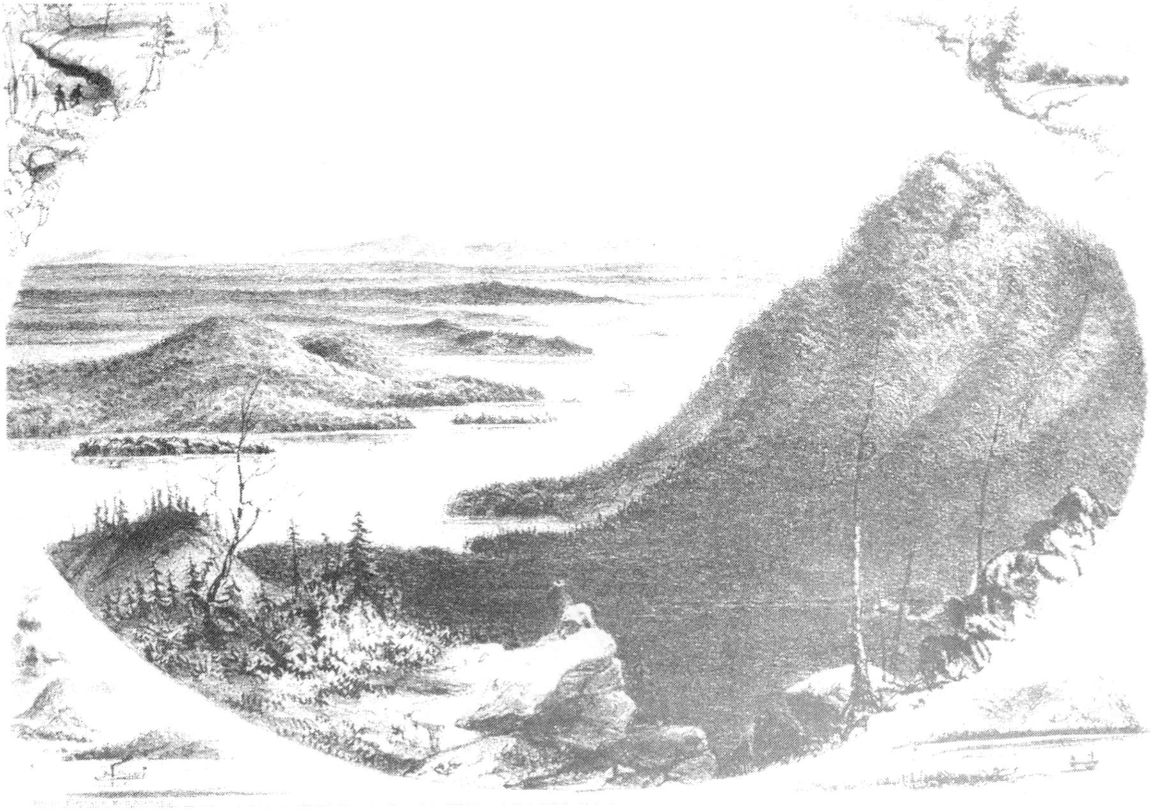

PLATE 37

VIEW OF OWLS HEAD FROM SUGAR LOAF MOUNTAIN

Plate 38 — The Pinnacle Looking North From the Little Lake, 1860

This small Lake lies in the southern part of the Township of Barnston, about ten miles east of Stanstead Plain. It is surrounded on all sides by mountains, of which the principal is called "Pinnacle Mountain." This eminence rises abruptly from the north-east shore of the Lake. The portion nearest the Lake rises to the height of 1000 feet nearly perpendicular from its base.

The view in the illustration is taken from the south end of the Lake, looking north.

W. S. Hunter, Jr., 1860

PLATE 38

THE PINNACLE, LOOKING NORTH FROM ...

Plate 39 — CONFLUENCE OF THE MASSAUWIPPI WITH RIVER ST. FRANCIS, 1860

This view is taken from a point opposite Lennoxville, affording a view of the junction of the two Rivers, St. Francis and Massawippi, college-hill and the bridge across the Massawippi forming the background. To the left, Bishop's College and a brick Chapel in Gothic style, present a commanding and imposing appearance. At the right, a short distance from the bank of the river, is situated the beautiful village of Lennoxville.

W. S. HUNTER, JR., 1860

PLATE 30

CONFLUENCE OF THE MASSAWIPPI WITH RIVER SAINT FRANCIS

at Lennoxville College, Lower Canada

Reproduced 1913

Plate 40 — RIVER ST. FRANCIS NEAR RICHMOND AND MELBOURNE, 1860

This view is one of the first seen by the tourist on approaching the Townships proper from Montreal, via the Grand Trunk Railway, and is the more pleasing as it contrasts with the rather uninteresting country between St. Hyacinthe and this point. The large building in the distance is St. Francis College, now affiliated with the McGill College, Montreal. The Quebec and Richmond Railway connects with the main line of the Grand Trunk at this place. Portions of Melbourne and Richmond are seen in the distance.

W. S HUNTER, JR., 1860

PLATE 4

College in the distance. Eastern Townships, C.E.

Plate 41 — VIEW ON THE RIVER SAINT FRANCIS, C.E., 1860

This view is taken from the garden of Mr Bowen, looking in a northerly direction
This is only one of the very many beautiful and highly picturesque views which may be had
along the charming River St. Francis. This river, though comparatively short, is excelled by
very few on this continent in the beauty of its views. From its source to its termination,
it exhibits one continued series of the most delightful and varied scenery.
The Grand Trunk Railway, which passes along at this point, forms the foreground
of the picture.

W. S Hunter, Jr., 1860

PLATE 41

VIEW ON THE RIVER WEAR, DURHAM.

Looking North East to the Residence of C.F.I. &c.

PLATE 42 — OWLS HEAD, ROUND ISLAND, WHET STONE ISLAND, AND
MAGOON POINT, 1860

This view embraces an important part of the scenery of the lake. The spectator
is supposed to be standing at a point about half a mile north of Harvey's Landing
looking across the Lake, with Round Island near the opposite shore, and Whetstone Island
nearest him. Among the mountains on the opposite shore, Owl's Head towers aloft,
in form like a cone, and its sides presenting gentle slopes to the north and the south. To the
right is seen Magoon's Point, its shores beautifully skirted with woods, and its background
finely diversified with meadows, corn-fields, and farm-houses.

W. S. HUNTER, JR., 1860

PLATE 42

Plate 43 — MOUNTAIN SCENERY, EASTERN TOWNSHIPS, C.E., 1860

Among the mountains of the west shore of Lake Memphremagog, Owl's-Head towers pre-eminent. In every view it is an object of grandeur. It is impossible to approach it from any point without exciting the deepest emotions of our nature. The journey to the top is comparatively easy, requiring about two hours to make the ascent
The background of our illustration is formed by the mountainous district which lies to the north-west of Owl's-Head, which prospect is truly sublime, mountain piled on mountains.

W. S HUNTER, JR, 1860

PLATE 43

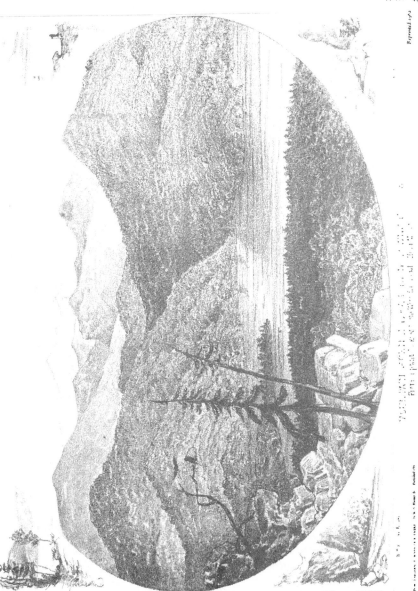

PLATE 44 — VIEW FROM SUGAR LOAF LOOKING NORTH LAKE MEMPHREMAGOG, 1860

This illustration, in connection with the view looking south from the same point, embraces nearly the whole lake. Lake Memphremagog has not inappropriately been called the Geneva of America. The beauty of some portions, and the splendid magnificence of other parts of its scenery, are no where else to be surpassed, — "custom cannot stale its infinite variety." Its bosom is picturesquely diversified by the islands which gem its surface. To the right, on the opposite shore of the lake, are situated the Townships of Stanstead, Hatley, Barnston, and Compton.

W. S HUNTER, JR., 1860

PLATE 44

VIEW FROM SUGAR LOAF LOOKING NORTH LAKE MEMPHREMAG :

Plate 45 — BISHOP'S COLLEGE, LENNOXVILLE, LOWER CANADA, 1865

In October 1864 Jasper Nicolls reported conversation with Lord Monk, Governor-General, and Galt, who was again Minister of Finance and added, "found the former very pleasant, and failed to get any encouragement from the latter." Financial difficulties continued. College had less than twenty students Bishop Williams mentioned possibility of University closing.

D. C. MASTERS, 1950

PLATE 45

BISHOP'S COLLEGE, LENNOXVILLE, LOWER CANADA.

Plate 46 — TOWN OF SHERBROOKE, 1867

Sherbrooke, the metropolis of the Eastern Townships of Canada, was incorporated a town in the year 1852. In extent of population, wealth, and commercial importance, it occupies the leading position in this portion of the Province. It is an active, enterprising place of about 4,500 inhabitants, delightfully situated at the confluence of the rivers St. Francis and Magog, on the south-eastern line of the Grand Trunk Railway, at a distance from Montreal of 96 miles. Divided by the latter stream, part of the town lies in the Township of Ascott and the remainder in Orford, Compton County, St. Francis District, of which district it is the chief lieu. The town is principally noted for its unsurpassed water-power and extensive manufactories. There are sixteen or eighteen mills and factories in constant operation, and others in course of erection. These embrace paper, woollen, grist, and saw mills, match, fuse, scythe, furniture, and sash factories, foundry and machine shops, &c. A large amount of capital is invested in most of these establishments, and a great many men, women, and children, from the skilled artisan to the common laborer, are employed in carrying them on.

EASTERN TOWNSHIPS GAZETTEER, 1867

PLATE 46

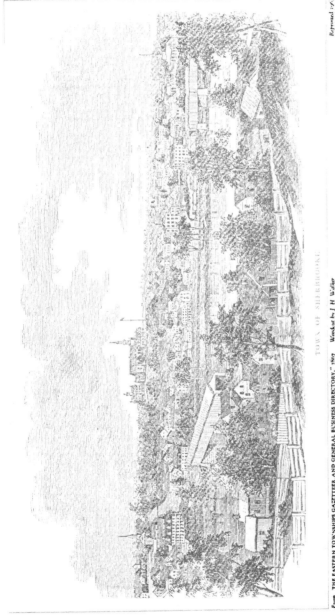

TOWN OF SHERBROOKE.

Woodcut by J. H. Walker

Reprinted 1862

From THE EASTERN TOWNSHIPS GAZETTEER AND GENERAL BUSINESS DIRECTORY," 1867

Plate 47 — PHILIPSBURG, 1867

*The village is prettily situated on the east side of
Missisquoi Bay, 46 miles south-east from Montreal It is
moderately elevated and declines towards the Bay, one of
the most beautiful sheets of water that can well be
conceived, abounding in fish of the finest varieties, while its
marshes afford excellent shooting It is generally admitted
to be one of the most desirable summer residences in the
Eastern Townships An extensive carriage manufactory
was established by J W. Eaton, in 1860, and continues in
successful operation. Some of the finest vehicles manufactured
in Canada are turned out of this establishment.*

EASTERN TOWNSHIPS GAZETEER, 1867

PLATE 47

PHILLIPSBURG, 1867

From "THE EASTERN TOWNSHIPS GAZETTEER AND GENERAL BUSINESS DIRECTORY,"   Reprinted 1962

Plate 48 — ESCARMOUCHE PRÈS DE COOK'S CORNERS, 1870

L'une de nos gravures représente le premier combat livré aux Féniens, lorsqu'ils traversèrent la frontière, le 25 mai dernier, dans la direction de Cook's Corners sous la conduite d'O'Neil. Les volontaires Canadiens, comme on le sait, avaient pris une excellente position sur une éminence qui leur offrait un abri d'où ils pouvaient mitrailler les Féniens. Ceux-ci, descendant la colline où ils avaient passé la nuit, furent assaillis à leurs premiers pas par une grêle de balles qui leur tua un homme et leur en blessa plusieurs. Nous avons donné, dans notre dernier numéro, des détails sur les autres événements de ce combat.

C'est la tombe de ce Fénien tué que nous offrons dans une autre gravure. Le pauvre Fénien fut enterré à dix-huit pouces sous terre et on éleva sur son cadavre un monument de grosses roches

L'OPINION PUBLIQUE, 9 JUIN 1870

PLATE 48

From "L'ORDRE PUBLIQUE," June 9, 1871

Reprinted 1962

PLATE 49

Reformed 1762

TOMBE DU PREMIER FENIEN TUÉ À CORNS CORNER, D'APRÈS PROVINCE, P.Q.

From "L'OPINION PUBLIQUE," June 9, 1870

Plate 50 — VOLUNTEER CAMP AT ECCLES HILL, 1870

Between 1866 and 1870 the British American Colonies were kept in a constant state of alarm by repeated rumours of Fenian Aggression. Finally on May 25, 1870 a body of 300, under "General" John O'Neill, crossed the border from Vermont, but was repulsed at Eccles Hill by a small force under Colonel Chamberlain. Later in the day, when Chamberlain had been reinforced, a second Fenian attempt upon the Hill was again repulsed.

PLATE 50

VOLUNTEER CAMP AT LOUIS HILL. From a sketch by A. Vogt

From "CANADIAN ILLUSTRATED NEWS," June 1, 1872

Reprinted 1962

PLATE 51

Reprinted 1962

From "THE FENIAN RAID OF 1870" — Wood engraving by John Henry Walker, 1877.

PLATE 52

From "L'OPINION PUBLIQUE", June 8, 1871.

Reprinted

Plate 53 — VILLAGE DE FRELIGHSBURG, 1870

Frelighsburg fut incorporé en village en septembre 1866. C'est un port d'entrée dans la paroisse de St-Armand Est, comté de Missisquoi — et est situé sur la rivière Pike. Il y a une tannerie et plusieurs magasins dans le village, un presbytère et une église anglicane, une école primaire et une école secondaire

EASTERN TOWNSHIPS GAZETTEER, 1867

PLATE 53

Reprinted 1882

From 'L'OPINION PUBLIQUE,' June 30, 1870

Plate 54 — VIEW FROM BELMERE,
LAKE MEMPHREMAGOG, 1870

*His Royal Highness Prince Arthur, after his final departure
from Montreal, passed a few days at Belmere,
the residence of Hugh Allan, on Lake Memphramagog
The scene shows in the background Owl's Head, one of
the loftiest mountains that inclose Lake Memphramagog. The
steam yacht "ORMOND" figures in the foreground,
moored to its wharf at the edge of the lake*
CANADIAN ILLUSTRATED NEWS, JULY 16, 1870

PLATE 54

VIEW FROM BELMERE, LAKE MEMPHREMAGOG

Plate 55 — A Distinguished Party at Belmere, 1870

Scene on the croquet ground at Belmere, with portraits of the visitors assembled
at the Villa during his Royal Highness Prince Arthur's stay, including the Prince,
Mr Hugh Allan, Miss Allan, Miss Starnes, Col. Earle and Lieut Picard

CANADIAN ILLUSTRATED NEWS, JULY 23, 1870

PLATE 55

A DISTINGUISHED PARTY AT RIMOUSKI

From "CANADIAN ILLUSTRATED NEWS," 1870

Reprinted 1963

Plate 56 — Dudswell Lower Lake and Stock Mountain, E.T., 1870

The county of Sherbrooke, in which is situated the township of Dudswell, is particularly rich in beautiful scenery, though a of tamer kind than is to be met with in many of the neighbouring counties. The general characteristic of the Sherbrooke scenery is low, flat ground, here and there gently undulating, and rising, in parts, into sloping hills, generally cultivated, and wearing a rich, pleasing aspect. In the vicinity of Orford, however, the country becomes uneven and broken, and presents ridges of highlands. Towards the head of the Connecticut river there are also numerous ridges of highlands, but with these exceptions the face of the country is generally level.

Canadian Illustrated News, October 1, 1870

PLATE 56

BIRCHELL LOWER LAKE AND STOCK BREEDING, I. L. Fox C. N.Y. P. & W.

Plate 57 — SHERBROOKE AND ST FRANCIS RIVER, LOOKING SOUTH, 1870

The pretty town of Sherbrooke, in the county of the same name, occupies an elevated situation on both banks of the River Magog, where it empties itself into the St Francis, at the point known as the Lower Locks. The St. Francis, one of the most winding of Canadian streams, after leaving Lake Weedon, passes through Dudswell, Bury and Westbury, enters the town of Ascot, where it takes a sudden turn to the north-west and sweeps past Lennoxville and Sherbrooke on its course into Lake St. Peter. The town one of the most thriving in the Eastern Townships, is situated on the line of the Grand Trunk, which passes for some little distance close by the river. It possesses valuable woollen and cotton manufactures and is the seat of the district courts

CANADIAN ILLUSTRATED NEWS, DECEMBER 24, 1870

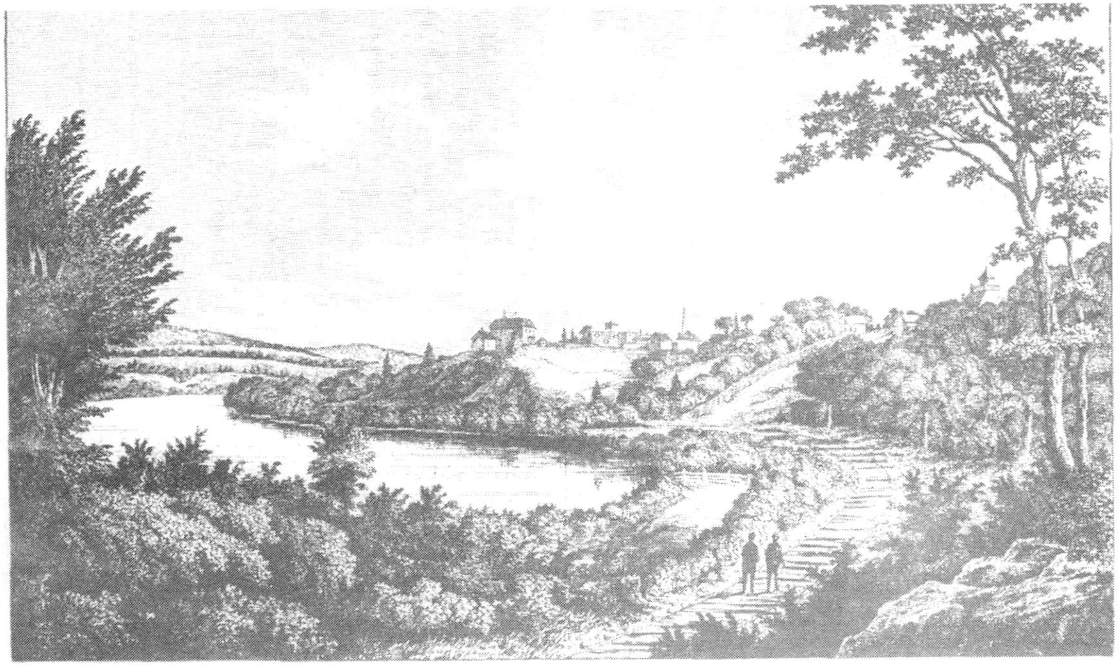

PLATE 57

From "CANADIAN ILLUSTRATED NEWS," December 24, 187?

Reprinted 1/2

Plate 58 — The Village of Robinson, E.T., 1871

Robinson is a small thriving village in the Township of Bury, Compton County (Eastern Townships), in the district of St. Francis, P.Q. It is twenty-one miles distant from Lennoxville, and forty-two miles from Lake Megantic. There is a daily mail and stage from Sherbrooke. A small creek, called Salmon Bank, runs through the village In the place are Church of England and Methodist Church, Town Hall, model school, grist and saw mills, etc

Canadian Illustrated News, February 11, 1871

PLATE 58

THE VILLAGE OF ROBINSON REEF, B.C. From a sketch by H. J. Warre

Plate 59 — View on the Magog River, Sherbrooke, 1871

The thriving town of Sherbrooke which skirts both banks of the Magog just before that stream falls into the St. Francis, is famous for its water-power, as well as for holding rank as the principal town in the Eastern Townships.

Canadian Illustrated News, February 18, 1871

PLATE 59

VIEW ON THE MAGOG RIVER, SHERBROOKE. From a Sketch by J.B. Roney

Plate 60 — SUNDAY LAKE, GARTHBY, E.T., 1871

This lake, which is also called Indian Lake, lies deeply among the hills, between
the townships of Garthby and Wolfestown, between two or three miles north-east
of Lake Nicolet, and about half a mile from the Quebec Road, from which however it is
not visible. It is about two miles long, and at its eastern end is connected by a short
stream, a few hundred yards in length, with another, somewhat longer lake, called
Breeches Lake. There are no clearances on either
The view is taken from the eastern or lower end of the lake, and the outlet is close on
the extreme right of the picture

CANADIAN ILLUSTRATED NEWS, MAY 20, 1871

PLATE 63

From *CANADIAN ILLUSTRATED NEWS*, *May 21, 1871*

Plate 61 — St Luke's Church, Waterloo, E.T., 1871

This handsome structure was lately opened for Divine
service by the Metropolitan the Bishop of Montreal.
It is thoroughly "Gothic" in style, built of
red and white brick
The interior is very fine, having a massive open roof,
the panels handsomely frescoed The principals of the roof are
from the manufactury of G. Roberts, the windows by
John Ostell, the pews from G. Wright, the stained glass
by J. C. Spence, all of Montreal
The organ is one of Messrs. Warren's best The architect
is Thomas Scott, Esq , Montreal. It has sittings for about
400, and, when completed, will cost $15,000 The roof
is covered with Melbourne and Granby slate,
blue and green

CANADIAN ILLUSTRATED NEWS, JUNE 17, 1871

PLATE 61

ST. LUKE'S CHURCH, WATERLOO, E. T.

From "CANADIAN ILLUSTRATED NEWS," June 17, 1871

Reprinted 1962

Plate 62 — Pont du Chemin à Lisses de Drummond et Arthabaska,
sur la Rivière Yamaska, 1871

Rivière Yamaska — Ce cours d'eau prend sa source dans le comté de Brome et arrose
une des vallées les plus riches du Canada, comprenant les comtés de Shefford,
Drummond, Saint-Hyacinthe, Richelieu et Yamaska. Il constitue le décharge de plusieurs
grands lacs et son cours atteint une longueur d'environ 90 milles. La rivière Yamaska
se jette dans le lac Saint-Pierre, à huit milles en aval de Sorel

Dictionnaire des Rivières et Lacs de la Province de Québec, 1914

PLATE 62

POST DE CHEMIN A LISSES DE DRUMMOND ET ATHABASKA, SUR LA RIVIERE CANADA

From "L'OPINION PUBLIQUE," September 17, 1871

Plate 63 — Les Chutes de la Rivière Yamaska Près de Cowansville, 1871

Ces chûtes se trouvent près de Cowansville joli village du township de Durham,
qui renferme environ six cents âmes. La rivière Yamaska arrose, comme l'on sait,
les townships de l'Est où elle a sa source près de la frontière américaine, passe devant
la ville de St. Hyacinthe et va se jeter à travers les comtés de Rouville et de Richelieu
dans le lac St. Pierre. Cette rivière est semée en quelque sortes de pouvoirs d'eau dont
quelques uns seulement sont exploités s'ils l'étaient tous comme ils devraient l'être, les
comtés quelle traverse et la ville de St. Hyacinthe seraient beaucoup plus riches

L'Opinion Publique, 2 novembre 1871

PLATE 63

LES CHUTES DE LA FERME VIMASSE, PRÈS DE DURAND DE LA CANTON DE L'EST

Plate 64 — VIEW OF LAKE NICOLET, FROM THE N.E., 1872

This lake lies chiefly in South Ham, county of Wolfe, Quebec, but is partly bordered on its north-west side by the township of North Ham. It is about four miles and a half long. It is the source of the River Nicolet, which flows from its south-western end. But though it thus gives rise to a considerable river, no streams have been discovered to enter it, except one tiny streamlet, about two feet wide, and an inch or two deep, so that it must be supplied by copious springs in the bottom of the lake. It is said, too, that if the water of the lake be raised only five feet above its ordinary level, as has happened occasionally in times of flood, the water will flow away from its north-east end, in a direction opposite to that of its usual outlet, the river Nicolet. The surplus water finds its way through the valley seen at the foot of the high hill on the left side of the drawing, into Lake Aylmer, and so to the River St. Francis.

CANADIAN ILLUSTRATED NEWS, MARCH 2, 1872

PLATE 24

Plate 65 — Bishop's University, Lennoxville, 1872

The College buildings are plain but commodious brick structures of the Elizabethan style, and consist of the principal's residence, lecture rooms, museum and library, dining hall and dormitories, and handsome college chapel. A convocation hall and grammar school more recently erected form another block of buildings in the same style. It is well situated on a picturesque slope rising above the confluence of the rivers St. Francis and Massawippi, and is in the centre of its grounds, consisting of about forty acres, which are under cultivation.

CANADIAN ILLUSTRATED NEWS, APRIL 27, 1872

PLATE 65

BISHOP'S UNIVERSITY, LENNOXVILLE, QUEBEC

From 'CANADIAN ILLUSTRATED NEWS', April 27, 1872

Plate 66 — A Sugar Bush (in the Eastern Townships), 1872

A pleasant and commonplace scene in the Eastern Townships in the spring of year.

CANADIAN ILLUSTRATED NEWS, MAY 11, 1872

PLATE 66

A SUGAR BUSH IN THE EASTERN TOWNSHIPS

Plate 67 — WINDSOR PAPER MILLS, P.Q., 1873

These mills are 83 miles from Montreal, on the Grand Trunk Railway between Portland
and Montreal. It is beautifully situated at the mouth of the Windsor River, at its junction
with the St. Francis. The large paper mill and wood pulp mill were built by Messrs.
Angus, Logan & Co., in 1866, and from some few houses, the place has grown
to be quite a large flourishing village. The mill has two fourdrinier paper machines
in it, and turns out four tons of paper daily. There are about 150 hands employed
about the works.

THE DOMINION GUIDE, 1873

PLATE 67

WINDSOR PAPER MILLS, P.Q.

From "THE DOMINION GUIDE," 1873   Wood engraving by Eugene Haberer

Plate 68 — WESLEYAN COLLEGE, STANSTEAD, P.Q , 1874

*In the winter of 1870 - 1871, a few Wesleyan ministers
met at Sherbrooke, P Q , and discussing topics relating
to the moral progress of the country, it was proposed to
start a plan for securing a college for the Eastern
Townships . . The first stockholders' meeting was held
in Stanstead, December 19, 1871, when the "Stanstead
Wesleyan College Association" was organized In October
1872, it was found that subscriptions to the amount of
$25,000 had been secured. . . The contract for the building
was awarded to G. W. Bryant, Esq , of Sherbrooke, . . .
December 24, 1875, the College was incorporated by Act
of the Provincial Parliament of Quebec*

B. F. HUBBARD, 1872

PLATE 68

WESLEYAN COLLEGE, STANSTEAD, P. Q.

From "FOREST AND CLEARINGS," 1874, by B. F. Hubbard, woodcut by J. Wiseman   Reprinted 1962

Plate 69 — LENNOXVILLE, Q. RUINS OF THE GRAMMAR SCHOOL,
BISHOP'S COLLEGE, 1874

The fire at the GRAMMAR SCHOOL, Lennoxville, was perceived by Mr. Livingstone Morris,
on his way to church, and he at once communicated his discovery to the congregation,
when a general stampede took place. On reaching the school, the flames were seen
bursting out round the cupola, and the fire had made such frightful progress that nothing
could be done to stop it. However, much useful work was done by tearing down the
wooden covered passage, leading from the school to the college, thereby preventing the spread
of the flames to the latter building. At the first alarm, Mr. Macfie (of the St. Francis &
Megantic International R. R.) rode over to Sherbrooke for the Merryweather engine, which
came with wonderful promptitude, and, though too late to prevent the spread of the fire,
did excellent service in saving the surrounding buildings. In fine, in less than three hours,
Bishop's College School was only represented by blackened and smouldering walls

CANADIAN ILLUSTRATED NEWS, FEBRUARY 14, 1874

PLATE (6)

LANARK HILLS. RUINS OF THE GRAMMAR SCHOOL, GEORGETOWN, 1874

From "CANADIAN ILLUSTRATED NEWS," February 14, 1874 — Wo... ...... by W. Schroer

Reprinted 1962

Plate 70 — Opening of the South Eastern Townships and
Kennebec R.R., 1874

On Thursday the 2nd ult., the Sherbrooke Eastern Townships & Kennebec Railway
was inaugurated with the customary ceremonies attendant on laying the first rail
and driving the first spike. This road runs from the active and ambitious town of Sherbrooke
where the inauguration took place, in a north easterly direction towards Quebec. It will
open up a large extent of fertile country, and is destined one day to become a great highway
of travel and traffic between the New England States and the Lower St. Lawrence.
The programme began at 4 p.m. with an address from the Vice-President of the road,
R. D. Morkill, Esq., Mayor of Sherbrooke, expressive of the pleasure of the Directors
at the success with which the work had been pushed, and of their hope that its
first section of 37 miles would soon be open

CANADIAN ILLUSTRATED NEWS, AUGUST 8, 1874

PLATE 70

OPENING OF THE SOUTH EASTERN TOWNSHIPS A.SSEMBLY HALL AT SHERBROOKE JULY 1

From 'CANADIAN ILLUSTRATED NEWS, *August 8, 1874 —* Wood engraving *by G. Gascard*

Reprinted 1963

Plate 71 — ORFORD MOUNTAIN, LAKE MEMPHREMAGOG, 1874

Lake Memphremagog has been called the Canadian Lake of Geneva, and is not undeserved of the name. Nestling among a cluster of mountains of no mean height, it offers many points of attraction to the artist and the tourist, and has already become a frequented place of resort in the summer Owl's Head and Orford Mountain are two of the principal features in the neighbourhood, several sketches of which were taken by Alfred Sandham at the time of the manufacturers' excursion. . .

CANADIAN ILLUSTRATED NEWS, SEPTEMBER 26, 1874

PLATE 71

OKFORD MOUNTAIN, LAKE MEMPHREMAGOG. AFTER A SKETCH BY H. SANDHAM

From "CANADIAN ILLUSTRATED NEWS," September 26, 1874 — Wood engraving by W. Schner

Reprinted 1962

PLATE 72

GREEN HEAD LAKE MEMPHREMAGOG. FROM A SKETCH BY THE MANAGER

From "CANADIAN ILLUSTRATED NEWS," September 26, 1874 — Wood engraving by W. Schuer

Reprinted 1962

Plate 73 — Opening of the S.E.T. & K.R.R., 1874

The formal opening of the Sherbrooke, Eastern Townships and Kennebec Railroad took place on Thursday, the 22nd ult. The celebration of the event took the form of an excursion from Sherbrooke to Lothrop's, in Westbury, a distance of fourteen miles, that being the length of road completed at the time. Some thousand persons took part in the excursion, filling ten cars, of which two were of the rolling stock of the new road. On arriving at their destination the party left the train and partook of refreshments. On the way back the train was stopped at Ascot Corners, where speeches were delivered by the Hon. Mr. Robertson, Treasurer of the Province of Quebec, and a number of other guests.

CANADIAN ILLUSTRATED NEWS, NOVEMBER 7, 1874

PLATE 73

OPENING OF THE SHERBROOKE

From "CANADIAN ILLUSTRATED NEWS," November 7, 1874 — Wood engraving by W. Sawyer

Reprinted 1962

PLATE 74 — EASTERN TOWNSHIPS — VIEW OF MOUNT ORFORD, 1875

Lake Orford, situated in Brome County at an altitude of 917 feet above sea level. Mount Orford situated to the north has an elevation of 2,860 feet. It is named after Orford Village, Suffolk, England

DICTIONARY OF RIVERS AND LAKES OF THE PROVINCE OF QUEBEC, 1914

PLATE 74

EASTERN TOWNSHIPS. VIEW OF MOUNT ORFORD AND PORT OF LAKE

From "CANADIAN ILLUSTRATED NEWS," May 29, 1875 — Wood engraving by W. S. Kent

Reprinted 1742

Plate 75 — BISHOP'S COLLEGE SCHOOL, LENNOXVILLE, 1875

The new School buildings of Bishop's College, Lennoxville, of which we give a representation elsewhere, have been erected during the past year to replace the former School House which was destroyed by fire on the 25th of January, 1874. During the intervening sixteen months, the School has been kept together in such temporary quarters as were at the time available, and it says something for the prestige of the School and for the College management that, despite the many discomforts and inconveniences experienced, the School roll for the last year numbered 100 boys. The year previous to the fire the number was 130, the whole available School accommodation being occupied, about 30 boys from the village and neighbourhood being non-resident, the old system of outside boarding houses having been discarded on the appointment of the present Rector. In the new School House accommodation is afforded for 110 boys, and with such a building it may be confidently expected that the School's former numbers will soon be reached again and perhaps surpassed.

CANADIAN ILLUSTRATED NEWS, JULY 17, 1875

PLATE 75

NEW SCHOOL BUILDINGS

BISHOP'S COLLEGE SCHOOL, LENNOXVILLE

ST. JOHN'S COLLEGE, CHELSEA

Plate 76 — SIMPSON TANNERY AND SAWMILL, DRUMMONDVILLE, P.Q., 1875

This is a sketch of Bonell's Tannery and Cook's Saw Mill at Drummondville,
on the South Eastern Railway. Four hundred tons of leather are manufactured at the former,
and two million feet of lumber sawn in the latter per annum. The railroad, which is
of great importance to this part of the Province, now connects Drummondville
with Sorel, and will, in about two weeks, be completed to Acton on the Grand Trunk.

CANADIAN ILLUSTRATED NEWS, DECEMBER 4, 1875

PLATE 76

SIMPSON TANNERY AND SAWMILL, FREDERICKSBURGH P.O. FROM A SKETCH BY MISS J. Y. COOKE

From "CANADIAN ILLUSTRATED NEWS," December 4, 1875

Reprinted 1962

Plate 77 — Drummondville, P.Q., 1876

The village of Drummondville, Que., is on the South Eastern Railway, 37 miles from Sorel and 17 miles from Acton, on the G.T.R. The depot is situated about one mile to the west of Mr. Bonnell's tannery and J. V. Cooke's Mill. Drummondville will soon be a place of some importance, as it is situated in the centre of a great lumbering district. The unrivalled water power on "Land Falls" on the St. Francis River some few hundred yards east of the depot will shortly be made desirable for manufacturing purposes.

CANADIAN ILLUSTRATED NEWS, MARCH 11, 1876

PLATE 77

DRUMMONDVILLE, P.Q.—From a Sketch by Mrs. J. V. Gorr.

From "CANADIAN ILLUSTRATED NEWS," March 11, 1876 — Wood engraving by W. S. hner

Reprinted 1/12

Plate 78 — DUDSWELL, THE LIME KILNS AND QUARRIES, 1876

The Dudswell Lime Kilns situated near the centre of the Township, County of Wolfe, shows the position they occupy, from a point south of the kilns. They stand about two miles from the Quebec Central Railway, which now runs forty-three miles from Sherbrooke and is intended to pass through to the city of Quebec. They are distant from Sherbrooke 24 miles, and the quality of the lime manufactured cannot be surpassed, according to an analysis made by Dr. Girdwood, of this city. There is 93 per cent. of pure lime in the stone, in its natural condition.

The quantity of limestone is unlimited, and is taken from a mountain distant about 100 feet from the kilns.

PLATE 78

BUDSWELL.— THE LIME KILNS AND QUARRIES.

From "CANADIAN ILLUSTRATED NEWS," October 14, 1876.

PLATE 70

EASTERN TOWNSHIPS: VALLEY OF THE ST. FRANCIS, NEAR SHERBROOKE

From "CANADIAN ILLUSTRATED NEWS," May 26, 1877 — Wood engraving by W. Schurr

Reprinted 1963

PLATE 80 — GREAT RAILWAY ACCIDENT, NEAR DANVILLE, QUEBEC, 1877

About 2 o'clock on the morning of the 12th inst., a railway accident occurred close to Danville station. It appears that some of the rear cars of a freight train became detached from the remainder of the train, being uncoupled on a grade, and ran backwards down the decline, where they were met by another freight train, following at some distance behind, causing a terrible collision. It is supposed that the driver and fireman of the other engine must have leaped off. The locomotive was a total wreck. Fourteen freight cars were also smashed up, and the debris scattered all over the line Only two men were reported badly injured One of them is a brakesman, and the other a man who had charge of a carload of horses, he sustained severe injuries, while the other man is badly scalded with water from the locomotive.

CANADIAN ILLUSTRATED NEWS. MAY 26, 1877

PLATE 80

Reprinted 1962

From 'CANADIAN ILLUSTRATED NEWS, May 26, 1877   Wood engraving by B. Schaur

Plate 81.— MOUNTFIELD, RESIDENCE OF MR. E. T. BROOKS, M.P., SHERBROOKE, 1878

The residence of Mr. Brooks, which is one of the most elevated sites in Sherbrooke, commands a magnificent view of the beautiful St. Francis River, as well as of the surrounding country, and is, without doubt, in every respect, the finest residence in Sherbrooke.

On entering the front hall, the preparations for the reception of the Vice-Regal party are seen on every hand. The vestibule is a miniature of Canadian curiosities, embracing among other things a black bear, a pure white goat skin from British Columbia, and a monster salmon, the latter a trophy, captured by Mr. Brooks on the Metis last summer.

CANADIAN ILLUSTRATED NEWS, AUGUST 24, 1878

PLATE 81

MOUNT STEPHEN RESIDENCE OF SIR G. T. BROWN, M.P. WINDSOR ST.

From "CANADIAN ILLUSTRATED NEWS," August 24, 1878

Reprinted 1962

Plate 82 — The Governor-General's Entry into Sherbrooke, 1878

The event of the week has been the triumphal advance of Lord and Lady Dufferin through the Townships — beginning at Richmond and closing at St. Johns. The daily papers have given full particulars which we need not repeat, but confine ourselves to the description of the reception at Mountfield. We are assured by the Sherbrooke Gazette that the preparations at Mountfield were on a scale commensurate with the honour conveyed in His Excellency's visit. The gateway to the grounds was spanned with an evergreen arch, over which appeared the motto "Cead Mille Faulthe." Close to the gateway and inside the enclosure, were pitched the tents of the military guard of honour (a self-imposed task, we understand, on the part of the military officers reading in Sherbrooke).

CANADIAN ILLUSTRATED NEWS, AUGUST 31, 1878

PLATE 82

From CANADIAN ILLUSTRATED NEWS," August 31, 1878

THE GOVERNOR-GENERAL'S PARTY AT THE GREENHOUSE

Plate 83 — THE ACCIDENT AT THE PAPER MILL, KINGSEY FALLS, P.Q., 1879

The employees and their friends were looking forward to their Christmas holiday; they had made arrangements for an evening of festivity, a supper and ball on New Year's Eve; in a moment when all seemed brightest and when no thought of possibility of danger was nigh, one of the large Pulp boilers, in use for reducing wood to pulp, suddenly exploded, instantly killing two men and wounding seven others; simultaneously with the explosion the buildings were seen to be on fire. For a moment, the men of the mill seemed stunned by the disaster, sorrow-stricken for the wounded men taken from the ruins; with loud voices they called the names of the missing men, and with herculean strength, tore parts of the burning building to pieces in their efforts to find the remains of the dead. A night of toil was spent in extraordinary efforts in the seemingly hopeless task of saving the Machine-Room department, and as much of the Pulp mill as possible, from the flames. Success rewarded their efforts with respect to the Machine Room department, but the Pulp mill, with all the large pieces of machinery contained in it, is a mass of ruins.

CANADIAN ILLUSTRATED NEWS, JANUARY 11, 1879

PLATE 83

Reproduced 1/2

THE ACCIDENT AT THE TISDR MILL, KNOWLES FALLS, P.Q.

From CANADIAN ILLUSTRATED NEWS, January 11, 1879. — Wood engraving by Eugène Hébert

Plate 84 — WATERLOO, P.Q., ACCIDENT ON THE SOUTH EASTERN RAILWAY, 1879

There was a fatal collision between the regular passenger train of the South Eastern Railway, bound for Acton and Sorel and the engine of a construction train, at Waterloo, P.Q., on the morning of the 26th June, at half past seven. The regular train had left the Waterloo Depot and proceeded about half a mile, when it collided with an engine running backwards at great speed to reach the station in time to avoid that train. The two engines came together round a curve. The engineer and fireman of the regular train jumped off and saved their lives. The crew of the other engine, John Daly and his fireman, Mouse Norreau, were killed instantly...

CANADIAN ILLUSTRATED NEWS, JULY 12, 1879

PLATE 84

STERLING P. Q.—ACCIDENT ON THE NEW PROVINCE RAILWAY

Reproduced 1/2

Plate 85 — View of Mount Elephantus from Fern Hill, 1879

The country about Lake Memphramagog has been termed the Switzerland of Lower Canada . . . For scenery the locality is unexcelled, while for summer recreation its facilities by rail and water are every year more appreciated.

CANADIAN ILLUSTRATED NEWS, JULY 19, 1879

PLATE 85

VIEW OF MOUNT ELEPHANTIS FROM PELY BEG, LAKE MEMPHREMAGOG

Reprinted 1962

Plate 86 — NICOLET RIVER, RAVINE BELOW BRIDGE
AND FARWELL'S MILL, 18 79

*The source of the Nicolet River is from the lake bearing
the same name, in the township of Ham, County of Wolfe.
It flows through the townships of Ham, Chester,
Arthabaska, Warwick, Bulstrode, Horton and Aston before
it empties into Lake St. Peter, three miles from the City
of Nicolet. There are two branches designated as the West
and the East. Its length is 60 miles and it covers a superficial
area of 1336 square miles*

DICTIONARY OF RIVERS AND LAKES OF THE
PROVINCE OF QUEBEC, 1914

PLATE 86

RAVINE OF THE NICOLET RIVER BELOW NICOLET BRIDGE.   FARWELL'S MILL ON NICOLET RIVER ABOVE THE BRIDGE.

From "CANADIAN ILLUSTRATED NEWS," *November 15, 1879*   *Reprinted 1962*

Plate 87 — BRIDGE OVER NICOLET RIVER, P Q

Nicolet River, named after Jean Nicolet, the famous
interpreter and explorer. In 1609, it was named
"du Pont" by Champlain after his friend Pont Gravé. It is
uncertain when the latter name was replaced by the
present one, but it was prior to 1672, as it is so designated in
acts of concessions of that date, later it was called
successively "Laudia" and "Cresse" after two seigneurs;
finally the name Nicolet was restored

GEOGRAPHIC BOARD OF CANADA, NINTH REPORT, 1911

PLATE 87

BRIDGE OVER NICOLET RIVER, P.Q.

From "CANADIAN ILLUSTRATED NEWS," November 15, 1879

Reprinted 1962

Plate 88 — GEORGEVILLE, P.Q., FROM A POINT SOUTH OF THE VILLAGE, 1880

A pleasant village situated on the East bank of Memphremagog in the township of Stanstead. The mountainous scenery renders the place attractive and picturesque. There is excellent fishing in the large and beautiful lake along which the village lies. A steamboat runs from Georgeville to Potton and Knowlton. The steamer Mountain Maid runs daily from Newport, Vt., to Magog. There are two churches in the village, Church of England, and Methodist; two good hotels, and a couple of stores. There are thirty schools in the township A great number of fine residences have been of late erected by gentlemen from Montreal, who spend the summer months in the place.

EASTERN TOWNSHIPS GAZETTEER, 1867

PLATE 88

BROCKVILLE, P. Q., FROM A POINT SOUTH OF THE VILLAGE, LOOKING NORTH. — Wood engraving by Eugene Haberer

From "CANADIAN ILLUSTRATED NEWS," July 17, 1885. (Quebec 187-)

Plate 89 — GEORGEVILLE, FROM THE HILL, LOOKING ACROSS THE LAKE, 1880

Lake Memphramagog is situated in the counties of Brome and Stanstead and partly in the State of Vermont It is thirty miles long and one to four miles wide, and empties into the St. Francis River at Sherbrooke, through the Magog River. Small steamers run a regular service between Newport, Vermont and Magog, situated at the extreme north of the lake.

It is fed by three small rivers in Vermont and numerous flows in Canada, the principal being the Cherry River. Its altitude is 682 feet above sea level.

DICTIONARY OF RIVERS AND LAKES OF THE PROVINCE OF QUEBEC, 1914

PLATE 89

GEORGEVILLE FROM THE HILL, LOOKING ACROSS THE LAKE TO GIBRALTAR POINT AND BALTON CLIFFS ON THE WEST SIDE

VIEWS ON LAKE MEMPHREMAGOG.—From Sketches by W. S. Hunter

Plate 90 — The Residence of J. B. Shurtliff, Esq., Hatley, T P., 1881

Shurtliff, J. B., *Farmer, residing on Lot 2, Con. 8 and owning 500 acres, worth $10,000. He holds the appointments of J.P. and Captain in the Militia, and for some time was a member of the Municipal Council. He has lived in the country since the year of his birth, 1807. P.O. address, Ayer's Flat*

BELDEN ILLUSTRATED ATLAS OF THE DOMINION OF CANADA, 1881

PLATE 9

THE RESIDENCE OF J. B. SHIRTLIFF, ESQ.

Plate 91 — Res and Mills of G. K. Nesbitt, Cowansville, 1881

Nesbitt, G. K., mill owner Has extensive mill property in Frelighsburg and Cowansville Was Mayor for 2 years Came to this county in 1869 Was born in Huntingdon Co P O address, Cowansville.

Belden Illustrated Atlas of the Dominion of Canada, 1881

PLATE 91

RES. AND MILLS OF G . K . NESBITT , CRANBVILLE , MISSISQUOI CO. QUE

From " BELDEN ILLUSTRATED ATLAS OF THE DOMINION OF CANADA," 1881

Reprinted 1962

Plate 92 — "Ferncliff," The Residence of W. G. Murray, Esq., Massawippi, 1881

Murray, W. G., gentleman, residing on Lot 7, Con. 5, of which he owns 17 acres. Born in the Province of Quebec, and settled here in 1875 P.O address, Massawippi. Belden Illustrated Atlas of the Dominion of Canada, 1881

PLATE 92

Plate 92

PLATE 93

From "BELDEN ILLUSTRATED ATLAS OF THE DOMINION OF CANADA," 1881

PLATE 94 — THE BEEBE PLAIN ADVENT CAMP GROUNDS, 1881

The Adventists have (at Beebe Plain) a fine camp ground of eight acres. At the eastern end is the "camp" consisting of about thirty frame buildings in the midst of which there is a quadrangle arranged with seats, and capable of accommodating a congregation of four thousand persons. The easterly part of the "grounds" is a prettily wooded dell, with winding walks.

BELDEN ILLUSTRATED ATLAS OF THE DOMINION OF CANADA, 1881

PLATE 94

THE BEEBE PLAIN ADVENT CAMP GROUNDS

From " BELDEN ILLUSTRATED ATLAS OF THE DOMINION OF CANADA," 1881

Reprinted 1972

Plate 95 — American House, G. T. Batchelder, Propr., Sweetsburg, 1881

Batchelder, G. T., *Proprietor of American House. Has also a Livery business. Residence P.O. address Sweetsburg Born in Brome Co Settled here December, 1878.*
Belden Illustrated Atlas of the Dominion of Canada, 1881

Plate 96 — Residence of John S. Campbell, Parish St Thomas, 1881

Campbell, J. S. and S. C., *owners of 520 acres in Lots 3, 4, 5, 10 and 13. in Cons 1, 2 and 3. Born in the Townships. J. S. Campbell is a J P. P.O address, Noyan*
Belden Illustrated Atlas of the Dominion of Canada, 1881

Plate 97 — Residence of Mrs. T. Lee Terrill, Stanstead Village, 1881

Terrill, late Hon. T. Lee, advocate and farmer. He owned over 1,000 acres in the province. Was M.P. and Provincial Secretary. Born in Sherbrooke, 1815. Married in 1850 to Miss Harriet Chamberlin, died August, 1879

Belden Illustrated Atlas of the Dominion of Canada, 1881

PLATE 97

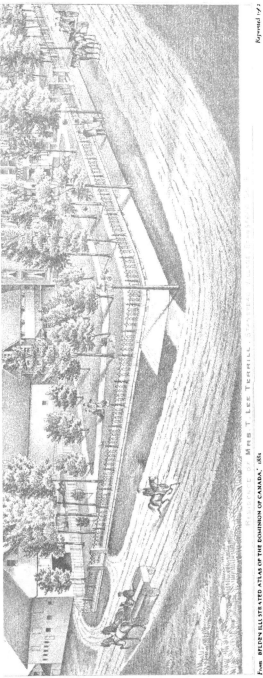

RESIDENCE OF MRS T. LEE TERRILL, STANTEAD, P.Q.

From BELDEN ILLUSTRATED ATLAS OF THE DOMINION OF CANADA, 1881

Reprinted 1973

Plate 98 — The Residence and Bank of J. C. Baker, Esq.,
Stanbridge East, 1881

Baker, J. C., banker in East Stanbridge. Was born in the State of Vermont, and came here in 1820.   Belden Illustrated Atlas of the Dominion of Canada, 1881

PLATE 68

Plate 99 — Residence of J. Brosseau, Esq, St. Armand, Missisquoi, 1881

Brosseau, J., Dep. — Collector of Customs, owns 7 acres, and resides on Lot 25 W.
Born 1842, at Longueuil. Came here in 1867. P.O address, St. Armand Station.
Belden Illustrated Atlas of the Dominion of Canada, 1881

PLATE 99

From BELDEN ILLUSTRATED ATLAS OF THE DOMINION OF CANADA," 1881

"RESIDENCE OF J. BROSSEAU Esq, ST EDWARD, MISSISQUE CO QUE"

Reproduced 1/2

Plate 100 — THE CAMPERDOWN, HOUSE AND RES. OF W. E. TUCK, ESQ.,
VILLAGE OF GEORGEVILLE, 1881

TUCK, W. E., *commercial traveller. He owns 193 acres in the townships.
Was born in the county in 1846 Residence and P.O. address, Georgeville.*
BELDEN ILLUSTRATED ATLAS OF THE DOMINION OF CANADA, 1881

PLATE 17

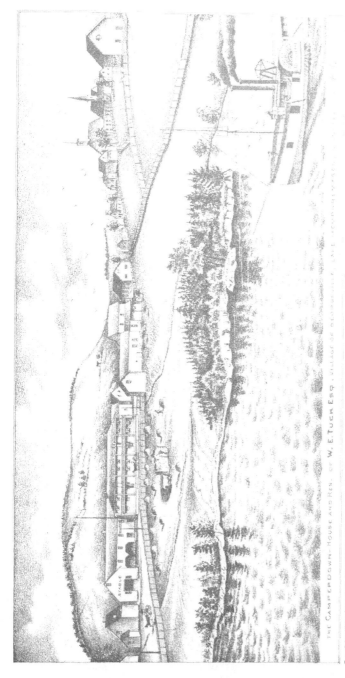

THE CAMPERDOWN. HOUSE AND RES. OF W. E TUCK ESQ. VILLAGE OF BEAVER DALE. LAKE SCUGOG ONTARIO

Reprinted 1962

From "BELDEN ILLUSTRATED ATLAS OF THE DOMINION OF CANADA," 1881

Plate 101 — The Residence of L. E. Parker, Esq., East Hatley, 1881

Parker, L. E., General merchant in Hatley Village, of which he is Secretary-Treasurer. Born in Canada 1830, and settled in the county same year. P.O. address, Hatley.

Belden Illustrated Atlas of the Dominion of Canada, 1881

PLATE I I

THE RESIDENCE OF L. E. PARKER ESQ.

From "BELDEN ILLUSTRATED ATLAS OF THE DOMINION OF CANADA," 1881

Plate 102 — BIRD'S EYE VIEW OF BEDFORD, P.Q., 1881

A brisk business village in Stanbridge Township, Missisquoi County, two miles east of the railway station known as Stanbridge depot. It is situated on Pike river, on which stream in the village and vicinity are several mills, foundries, &c., driving on active trade. Population of the place about 400 Distance from St. Johns, twenty miles; Sweetsburg, eighteen miles, and Philipsburg, eight miles Mails are received daily The Circuit Court for the county is held here, and it is also the headquarters of the Missisquoi Agricultural Society. There are two churches, Church of England and Methodist, an academy and district school. The scenery about here is very attractive, and the land of an excellent quality.

EASTERN TOWNSHIPS GAZETTEER, 1867

PLATE 2

Reprinted 1/2

By H. Wilks, Published by J. J. Sumer, Madison, Wisconsin, 1881

Plate 103 — Bird's Eye View of Coaticook, P.Q., 1881

A thriving village on the Coaticook river, and contiguous to Grand Trunk Railway, in the County of Stanstead. It is only nine miles from the State of Maine, and is one of the most important ports of entry in the Eastern Townships. There is a daily mail from Quebec and Montreal, and also from the South. There are three passenger trains daily each way. The stage leaves on arrival of the train every evening for Stanstead, and returns in the morning to connect with train going to Montreal. There are four churches in the village — Church of England, Roman Catholic, Baptist, and Methodist, two district schools, one high school, under the superintendence of the first-named Church. There are a foundry, saw, and grist mill, sash, door, match, and mowing machine factories, besides several other manufacturing establishments.

EASTERN TOWNSHIPS GAZETTEER, 1867

By H. Weber. Published by J. J. Stoner, Madison, Wisconsin, 1881

Plate 104 — Bird's Eye View of Lennoxville, P.Q., 1881

A village very attractively situated at the junction of the Massawippi and St. Francis
Rivers, on the line of E. T. Railway, three miles south-west of Sherbrooke
It has a population of about 600. Mails are received twice each day from Montreal, (which is
distant about 100 miles), and once a day from other directions There is a good deal
of activity observable in this village, trade is lively, and the number of persons who visit
the place, especially in summer, is large. There are two churches, two large hotels, and
a great many stores and shops in the place

EASTERN TOWNSHIPS GAZETTEER, 1867

PLATE 104

LENNOXVILLE P.Q.
1881

By H. Wellge. Published by J. J. Stoner, Madison, Wisconsin, 1881

Reprinted 1952

Plate 105 — Bird's Eye View of Derby Line, Vt. and Rock Island, P.Q., 1881

Was formerly and for municipal purposes is still a portion of Stanstead Plain village. It is separated from the older settlement by a high range of hills, but it is in the same village municipality, though it has a distinct post office. It is an active trading and manufacturing place with a population of about 400, or 1100 or 1200 including Stanstead. Mails are received and dispatched daily.

Eastern Townships Gazetteer, 1867

PLATE 108

Vignette

By H. Weir, Published by J J Sawyer, Malham, Wakesmann, 1881

Plate 106 — BIRD'S EYE VIEW OF SHERBROOKE, P.Q., 1881

Sherbrooke, the metropolis of the Eastern Townships of Canada, was incorporated a town in the year 1852. In extent of population, wealth, and commercial importance, it occupies the leading position in this portion of the Province. It is an active, enterprising place of about 4,500 inhabitants, delightfully situated at the confluence of the rivers St. Francis and Magog, on the south-eastern line of the Grand Trunk Railway, at a distance from Montreal of 96 miles. Divided by the latter stream, part of the town lies in the Township of Ascot and the remainder in Orford, Compton County, St. Francis District, of which district it is the chief lieu. The town is principally noted for its unsurpassed water-power and extensive manufactories. There are sixteen or eighteen mills and factories in constant operation, and others in course of erection. These embrace paper, woollen, grist, and saw mills; match, fuse, scythe, furniture, and sash factories, foundry and machine shops, &c. A large amount of capital is invested in most of these establishments, and a great many men, women, and children, from the skilled artizan to the common laborer, are employed in carrying them on.

EASTERN TOWNSHIPS GAZETTEER, 1867

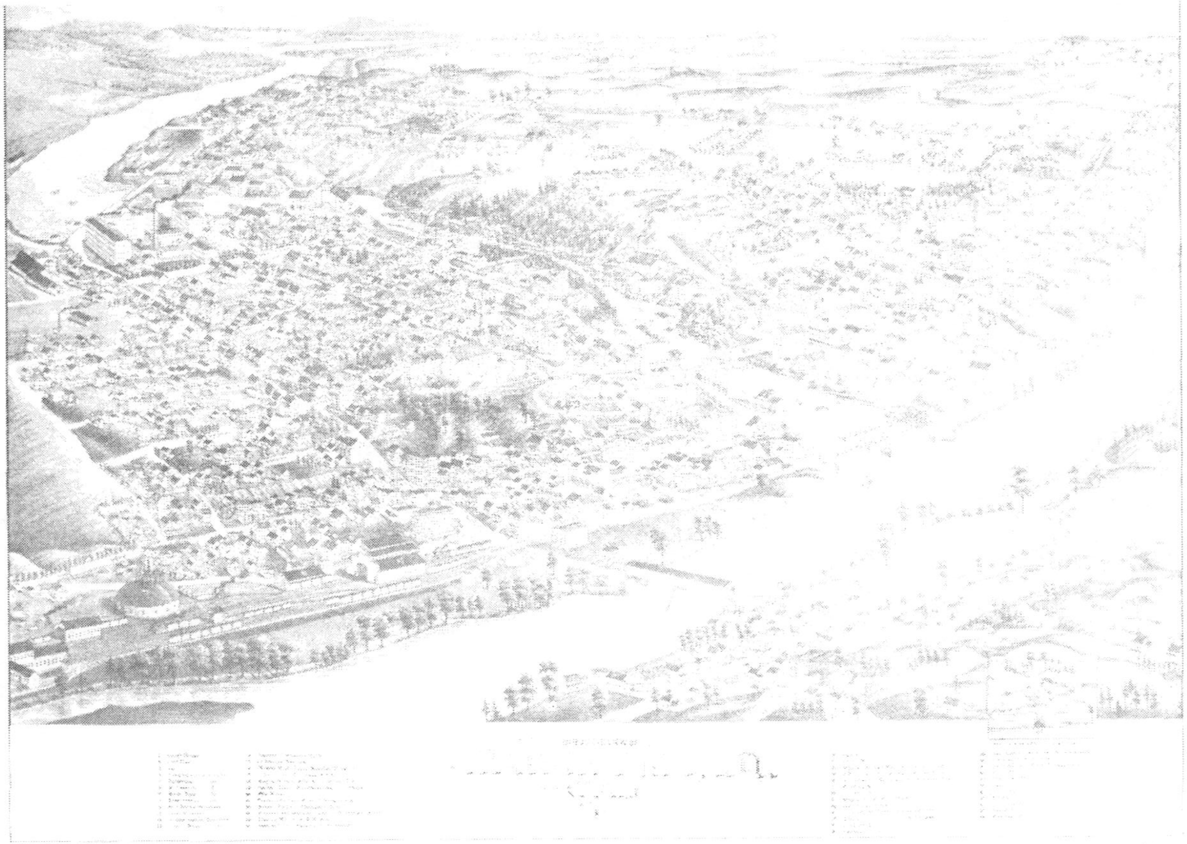

PLATE 106

R. H. Welge, Published by J. J. Stoner, Madison, Wisconsin, 1889

Plate 107 — BIRD'S EYE VIEW OF WATERLOO, P.Q., 1881

An energetic and flourishing village in the township and county of Shefford, situated on the line and near the terminus of the Stanstead, Shefford, and Chambly Railway. It was incorporated in the fall of 1866. The population, which is steadily on the increase, is now estimated at 1500. The amount of trading and manufacturing business done is large for a place of its size. There are several well stocked stores, from which the people for miles around derive their supplies. In the way of manufactures, there are a large tannery, iron foundry, saw and grist mills, furniture and carriage shops, &c. There are also a branch of the Eastern Townships Bank, and an office of the Montreal Telegraph Company in the village. There are four churches, Church of England, Roman Catholic, Wesleyan Methodist, and Advent, an excellent academy for male and female pupils, which is liberally supported, French and English district school, besides two private schools.

EASTERN TOWNSHIPS GAZETTEER, 1867

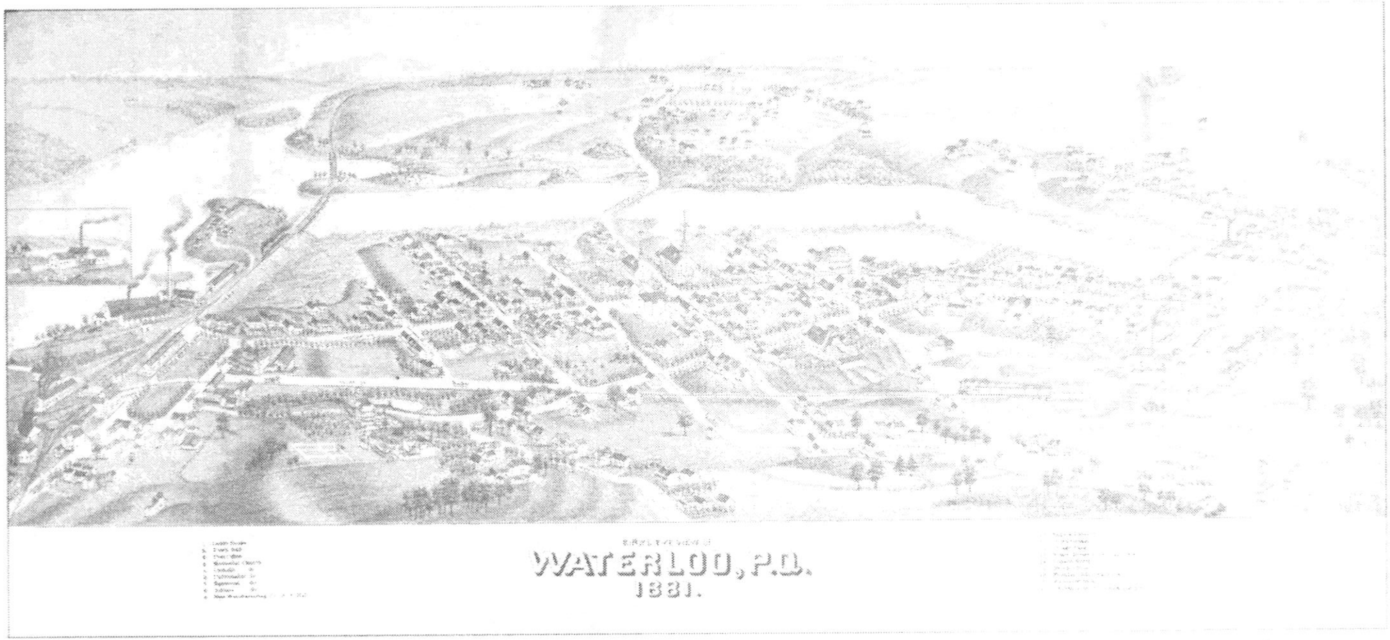

PLATE 17

WATERLOO, P.O.
1881.

By H. Willis, Published by J. J. Stoner, Madison, Wisconsin, 1881

Reprinted 1962

Plate 108 — Three Views in the Life of
a Canadian Farmer, 1881

*A very interesting portrayal of homesteading over
a period of thirty years.*

PLATE 18

THREE VIEWS IN THE LIFE OF A CANADIAN FARMER
IN THE EASTERN TOWNSHIPS

NO. 1—THE SHANTY IN THE BUSH

NO. 2—FIFTEEN YEARS AFTER SETTLEMENT

NO. 3—THIRTY YEARS AFTER SETTLEMENT

From "THE EASTERN TOWNSHIPS—INFORMATION FOR INTENDING SETTLERS," 1881   *Reprinted 1/2*

Plate 109 — View of the Town of Granby, 1881

The beautiful town of Granby, one of the pleasantest spots in the Eastern Townships One of its principal industries is the Granby Rubber Factory, said to be without exception one of the best appointed of its kind in America. Its capital is Canadian, and it employs between 40 or 50 hands, with as many orders as it can fill. Its speciality is Gossamer rubber clothing, made up in fine quantities. These goods are warranted equal in quality and finish to any made in the United States.

CANADIAN ILLUSTRATED NEWS, MARCH 17, 1883

PLATE 109

Major Robert Rogers

*Leader of expedition against the Abenakis
at St Francis in 1759*

Colonel Benedict Arnold

*Commander of the Revolutionary Forces that
followed the Kennebec Road and Arnold River
to Quebec*

Robert Rogers (1731 - 1795) was born in Dumbarton, New Hampshire in 1731, the second son of James Rogers and Mary McFatridge. In 1755 he organized a company of scouts, known as Roger's Rangers, for service against the French. He served throughout the Seven Years War. In 1760 he was commissioned to take possession of the Western Lake Posts. At the outbreak of the American Revolution he organized the Queen's Rangers, and later in 1779, the King's Rangers. He died in London, England on May 18, 1795.

Benedict Arnold (1741 - 1801) was born at Norwich, Connecticut on January 14, 1741, the son of Benedict Arnold and Hannah Waterman. He saw service in the Seven Years War, and was one of the first militia officers to enlist in the Revolutionary Army in 1775. He was co-commander with Ethan Allan of the force which captured Ticonderoga May 10, 1775. After Montgomery's death, Arnold succeeded to the command of the American Forces invading Canada, and conducted their retreat in 1776. In 1779 he became a traitor to the revolutionary cause. He died in London, England on June 14, 1801. Two of his sons settled in Upper Canada on land granted to him in 1791.

Major-General James Wolfe
(1727 - 1759)
After whom Wolfe County was named

Charles Gordon Lennox
The Fourth Duke of Richmond (1764-1819)
After whom Richmond and Lennoxville
were named

James Wolfe (1727 - 1759) was born at Westerham, Kent, England, January 2, 1727, the son of Colonel Edward Wolfe. In 1758 he was appointed a Brigadier-General in the expedition against Louisbourg, in 1759 at the age of thirty-two years William Pitt appointed him to command the expedition against Quebec with the rank of Major-General. The conquest of Quebec, September 13, 1759 cost him his life.

Charles Gordon Lennox, fourth Duke of Richmond, (1764 1819), Governor General of Canada 1818 - 1819 The only son of Lord George Henry Lennox and Louisa, daughter of the fourth Marquis of Lothian In 1818 he was appointed Governor General of Canada He died of hydrophobia from the bite of a pet fox, near Richmond, Upper Canada, on August 28, 1819

Sir John Coape Sherbrooke
After whom the City of Sherbrooke was named

Sir John Coape Sherbrooke (1764 - 1830) was born in England in 1764, the third son of William Coape, J P., of Farnah in Duffield, Derbyshire, who took the name of Sherbrooke on his marriage in 1756 to Sarah, one of the co-heiresses of Henry Sherbrooke, of Oxton, Nottinghamshire. In 1784 - 85 he was stationed in Nova Scotia, in 1811 he was appointed Lieutenant-Governor of Nova Scotia During the war of 1812 the defence of Nova Scotia was conducted by him with great success. In 1816 he became Governor of Canada. He died at Calverton, Nottinghamshire, on February 14, 1830. In 1811 he married Katherine, daughter of the Rev Reginald Pyndar, Rector of Madresfield, Worcestershire

Maj · Gen Frederick George Heriot
founder of Drummondville

Frederick George Heriot (1786 - 1843) was born in the Island of Jersey on January 11, 1786, the third son of Roger Heriot and Anne Nugent He came to Canada in 1802. He was second in command of the Canada Voltigeurs during the War of 1812 In 1816, he founded the Town of Drummondville In 1840 he was appointed a member of the Special Council of Lower Canada He rose to the rank of Major-General in the Army. He died at Drummondville on December 29, 1843

George Jehoshophat Mountain
(1789-1863)
third Anglican Bishop of Quebec

Mgr Antoine Racine
(1822-1893)
Evêque de Sherbrooke

George Jehoshophat Mountain (1789 - 1863) third Anglican Bishop of Quebec (1837 - 1863) was born at Norwich, England, on July 27, 1789, the second son of the Right Reverend Jacob Mountain. He was admitted to Holy Orders in 1814. In 1836, he was appointed Bishop of Montreal, and in 1837 Bishop of Quebec. This See he administered until his death at Quebec in 1863. In 1814 he married Mary Hume and by her he had several children. In 1853 he was made a D.C.L. of Oxford University.

Antoine Racine (1822 - 1893) first Roman Catholic Bishop of Sherbrooke, was born at Jeune Lorette, near Quebec, Lower Canada, on January 26, 1822, was educated at Quebec, and was ordained a priest in 1844. He was made first Bishop of Sherbrooke in 1874, and he presided over this See until his death, at Sherbrooke, Quebec, on July 17, 1893.

Hon. Sir Alexander Tilloch Galt
(1817-1893)

Hon. John Henry Pope
(1819-1889)

Sir Alexander Tilloch Galt (1817-1893) was born in Chelsea, London on September 6, 1817, the youngest son of John Galt, the Scottish novelist. He came to Canada in 1835 as a clerk in the office of the British American Land Company at Sherbrooke, and from 1844 to 1855 was commissioner of the Company. In 1849 he was elected to the Legislative Assembly of Canada for Sherbrooke County as an independent, but he resigned in 1850. He was returned for the Town of Sherbrooke in 1853; and he continued to represent this constituency in the Assembly until 1867, and in the House of Commons until 1872. He was one of the chief architects of the British North America Act and one of the Fathers of Confederation. In 1867 he became the first Minister of Finance of the Dominion. In 1880 he was appointed the first Canadian High Commissioner in London. He was married in 1848 to Elliott, daughter of John Torance and in 1851 to her younger sister, Amy Gordon. By his first wife he had one son; and by his second wife, two sons and eight daughters. He was created a K.C.M.G. in 1869, and a G.C.M.G. in 1878. He died at Montreal on September 19, 1893.

Born in the township of Eaton (now Cookshire) December 19, 1819, the son of John Pope and Sophia Laberee. He was educated at Cookshire school, and first devoted himself to agriculture. In 1857 he was elected to represent Compton as a Liberal-Conservative in the Legislative Assembly of Canada. He represented this constituency continuously, first in the Assembly and then in the House of Commons, until his death in 1889. In 1871 he was sworn of the Privy Council and became Minister of Agriculture. He resigned at the time of the "Pacific Scandal" in 1873, but he was one of the chief lieutenants of Sir John A. Macdonald in opposition. In 1878, when Macdonald came back to power, he resumed his old portfolio. In 1885 he took over the Ministry of Railways and Canals. He married in 1845 and had three children.

He was one of the original promoters of the Eastern Townships Bank, the most ardent promoter of the International Railway, and one of the original partners of the Paton Manufacturing Company of Sherbrooke. It is very difficult to mention any major development in the Eastern Townships in which he was not involved in a constructive manner.

Plate 120 — EASTERN TOWNSHIPS VIEWS ON
HISTORICAL CHINA

*Frances Morley & Company of Staffordshire, England
(circa 1847) reproduced two of the W H Bartlett views of
the Eastern Townships on what is now known as
"Canadian Historical China." They are exceptionally
attractive and very worthy of inclusion in a pictorial record
of the District.*

PLATE 12.

CREAM JUG   "GEORGEVILLE" TEAPOT   TEA CUP

See Plate 16

"OUTLET OF LAKE MEMPHREMAGOG"

PLATTER

See Plate 17

Plate 121 — BILLS OF EARLY EASTERN
TOWNSHIPS BANKS

*The Provincial Bank received its charter in 1856, having its
one and only office in Stanstead. It closed its doors in 1862.
The Eastern Townships Bank was backed by local
business men and received its charter in 1859. Its head office
was in Sherbrooke, and agencies were established in
Stanstead and Waterloo. The first President was
Col. Benj. Pomeroy*
*The bank from its inception was accepted by the general
population and its policies gave the impetus for the
substantial growth throughout the Townships which
followed*

PLATE 121

BILLS OF EARLY EASTERN TOWNSHIP BANKS

BIBLIOGRAPHICAL REFERENCES
OF THE EASTERN TOWNSHIPS

ADAMS, C.   Thetford Mines. Historique et biographies .   Thetford Mines, 1929

BARTLETT, W. H , AND N P. WILLIS.   Canadian scenery illustrated .   London, 1842 2v.

BELDEN, H., & Co.   Illustrated atlas of the Dominion of Canada .   Toronto, 1881.

BOUCHETTE, JOSEPH   A topographical description of the Province of Lower Canada   London, 1815

BOUCHETTE, JOSEPH.   The British Dominions in North America ... London, 1832 2v

BOUCHETTE, JOSEPH.   A topographical dictionary of the Province of Lower Canada   . London, 1832

BRITISH AMERICAN LAND COMPANY.   Information respecting the Eastern Townships of Lower Canada .   London, 1833.

BRITISH AMERICAN LAND COMPANY.   Views in Lower Canada   .. London, 1836.

BUGEIA, JULIA H. S , AND T. C. MOORE   In old Missisquoi ... Montreal, 1910

BULLOCK, WILLIAM BRYANT.   Beautiful waters .   . Newport, Vt , 1926.

CAMPBELL, FRANCIS WAYLAND   The Fenian invasions of Canada ... Montreal, 1904.

CANADA.   First report of the special committee ... Settlement of the Eastern Townships of Lower Canada ...
    Toronto, 1851.

CANADA.   Subdivisions du Bas-Canada en paroisses et townships ... Quebec, 1853.

CANADA.   Subdivisions du Bas-Canada en paroisses et townships depuis 1853 ... Quebec, 1860.

CANADA   The Eastern Townships. Information for intending settlers ... Ottawa, 1881.

CANADIAN ILLUSTRATED NEWS   Montreal, 1869 - 1883

CARON, IVANHOE.   Les Cantons de l'Est, 1791 - 1815 ... Quebec, 1927

CHANNELL, L S.   History of Compton County ... Cookshire, Que., 1896.

CHAREST, F. V.   Notes sur la paroisse de St. Janvier de Weedon ... Sherbrooke, 1891

CHARTIER, J. B   La colonisation dans les Cantons de l'Est ... St. Hyacinthe, 1871.

CLEVELAND, EDWARD.   A sketch of the early settlement and history of Shipton, Canada East ... Richmond, 1858.

CONNINGHAM, FREDERICA A.   Currier & Ives prints ... New York, 1949.

CROCKER, WILLIAM P.   Report of the survey of the projected line of Railroad from Stanstead to Montreal ...
    Montreal, 1845.

DAY, MRS. C. M.   Pioneers of the Eastern Townships ... Montreal, 1863.

DAY, MRS. C. M.   History of the Eastern Townships ... Montreal, 1869.

DIX, JOHN ROSS.   A handbook for Lake Memphremagog ... Boston (1859)

DRAPEAU, STANISLAS.   Etudes sur le développement ... du Bas-Canada ... Quebec, 1863.

DRUMMOND, MAY H.   The grand old man of Dudswell ... Quebec, 1916.

EVANS, FRANCIS A.   The emigrants' directory and guide ... London, 1833.

THE FENIAN RAID OF 1870, BY REPORTERS PRESENT AT THE SCENES ... Montreal, 1870.

FOSTER, JOHN.   Report on the Phillipsburg, Farnham & Yamaska Railway ... St. Hyacinthe, 1872.

HUBBARD, B F.   Forests and clearings ... Montreal, 1874

HUNTER, WILLIAM S.   Hunter's Eastern Townships Scenery ... Montreal, 1860

HUTCHINSON, JOHN I.   Sir Alexander Tilloch Galt ... Toronto, 1930.

IRVING, L. H.   Officers of the British Forces in Canada, 1812 - 15 ... Welland, 1908.

JOLLIFFE, PERCIVAL.   Andrew Hunter Dunn ... a memoir ... London, 1919.

KINGSFORD, WILLIAM.   The history of Canada ... Toronto, 1887 - 1898 10v.

239

LEFEBVRE, P J   Monseigneur Antoine Racine . . . Sherbrooke, 1884

LOVELL, JOHN   The Canada Directory for 1857 - 58 . . . Montreal, 1857.

MCALEER, GEORGE   Reminiscent and otherwise . . . Eastern Townships . . . Worcester, 1901.

MCALEER, GEORGE   A study . . . Indian place names Missisquoi . . . Worcester, 1906.

MACDONALD, CAPT JOHN A.   Troublous times in Canada . . . Toronto, 1910.

MAGNAN, HORMISDAS   Dictionnaire historique . . . Quebec. Arthabaska, 1925.

MARTIN, R MONTGOMERY   History . . . of Upper and Lower Canada . . . London, 1838.

MASTERS, D. C.   Bishop's University, the first hundred years . . . Toronto, 1950.

MILLMAN, THOMAS R.   A short history of the Parish of Dunham . . . Granby, 1946.

MILLMAN, THOMAS R.   The life of the Right Rev. Charles James Stewart . . . London, Ont., 1953.

MISSISQUOI COUNTY HIST SOC.   The first report of . . . 1906.

MONTGOMERY, GEORGE H.   Missisquoi Bay   . . Granby, 1950.

MORRILL, V. E. AND E. G. PIERCE.   Men of today in the Eastern Townships . . . Sherbrooke 1917.

MOUNTAIN, ARMINE W.   A memoir of George Jehoshophat Mountain . . . Montreal, 1866.

MOUNTAIN, GEORGE JEHOSHOPHAT.   Songs of the wilderness . . . London, 1846.

NELSONVILLE, QUE   Programme of the jubilee celebration of the Parish of Nelsonville . . . (n.p. 1904.)

NOYES, J. P.   Sketches of some early Shefford pioneers . . . (n p., 1905.)

O'BREADY, MGR MAURICE.   Panoramas et gros plans . . . unpublished.

L'OPINION PUBLIQUE, JOURNAL ILLUSTRE. . . . Montreal, 1870 - 1883.

PARKMAN, FRANCIS.   The works of . . . Boston, 1897 - 98.

QUEBEC.   1894 Settlers' guide . . . Quebec, 1894.

ROUILLARD, EUGENE.   Noms geographiques de la Province de Quebec . . . Quebec, 1906.

ROY, PIERRE GEORGES.   Les noms geographiques de la Province de Quebec . . . Levis, 1906.

ROY, CHARLES JOSEPH.   Visite de S E. Mgr Stagni dans les Cantons de l'Est . . . Quebec, 1914.

SAINT-AMANT, JOSEPH CHARLES.   Un coin des Cantons de l'Est . . . Drummondville, 1932.

ST. AMANT, J C.   L'Avenir, Townships de Dunham et de Wickham . . . Arthabaskaville, 1896.

SETTLEMENT OF THE TOWNSHIPS OF LOWER CANADA.   (In: The Canadian Review and Literary & Historical Journal, No. 1, July, 1824 . . . Montreal, 1824)

SHORTT, ADAM AND A. G. DOUGHTY.   Canada and its provinces . . . Toronto, 1914.

SHUFELT, HARRY B   Along the old roads . . . Knowlton, 1956.

SMALL, H. B. AND J. TAYLOR.   The Canadian Handbook and tourists' guide . . . Montreal, 1866.

SMITH & Co., PUBL.   The Eastern Townships Gazetteer . . . St. Johns, 1867.

SPENDLOVE, F. ST. GEORGE.   The face of early Canada . . . Toronto, 1958.

SULTE, BENJAMIN, AND OTHERS.   A history of Quebec . . . Montreal, 1908. 2v.

TAYLOR, ERNEST M.   History of Brome County . . . Montreal, 1908 - 1937. 2v.

TERRILL, FRED'K. WM   A chronology of Montreal and of Canada . . . Montreal, 1893.

THOMAS, CYRUS.   Contributions to the history of the Eastern Townships . . . Montreal, 1866.

THOMAS, CYRUS.   The history of Shefford . . . Montreal, 1877.

TROUT, J. M AND EDW. TROUT.   The railways of Canada for 1870 - 1 . . . Toronto, 1871.

WALLACE, W. STEWART.   The Encylopedia of Canada . . . Toronto, 1935, 6v.

WALLACE, W. STEWART.   The Dictionary of Canadian biography . . . Toronto, 1945. 2v.

ZEILINSKI, S. A.   The story of the Farnham meeting . . . Fulford, P.Q , 1961.

By ORDER OF HIS EXC.

CAPTAIN GENERAL & GOVERNOR IN C...

REFERENCES

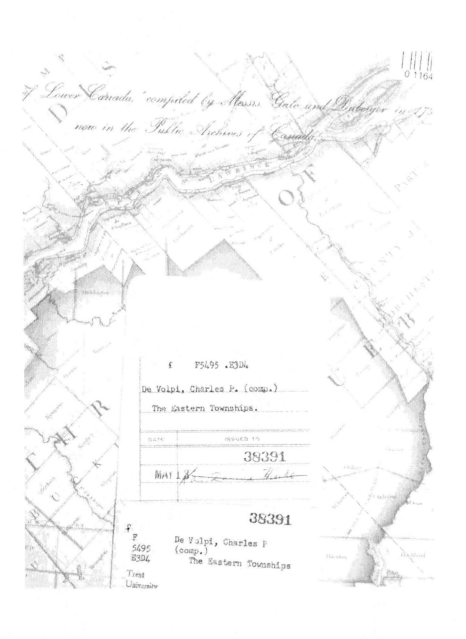

9 781014 049025